Crafting for CAT LADIES

Crafting for CAT LADIES

35 PURR-FECT FELINE PROJECTS

by Kat Roberts

New York

LARK
New York

An Imprint of Sterling Publishing Co., Inc.
1166 Avenue of the Americas
New York, NY 10036

Text © 2017 by Kat Roberts
Photography & illustrations © 2017 by Sterling Publishing Co., Inc.

ISBN 978-1-4547-1039-4

Distributed in Canada by Sterling Publishing Co., Inc.
c/o Canadian Manda Group, 664 Annette Street
Toronto, Ontario, Canada M6S 2C8
Distributed in the United Kingdom by GMC Distribution Services
Castle Place, 166 High Street, Lewes, East Sussex, England BN7 1XU
Distributed in Australia by NewSouth Books
45 Beach Street, Coogee, NSW 2034, Australia

For information about custom editions, special sales, and premium and corporate purchases,
please contact Sterling Special Sales at 800-805-5489 or specialsales@sterlingpublishing.com.

Manufactured in China

2 4 6 8 10 9 7 5 3 1

www.larkcrafts.com
www.sterlingpublishing.com

Photography by Chris Bain
Design by Shannon Nicole Plunkett
Illustrations by Julia Morris

Contents

Introduction

Considering there were times in history when cats were worshipped as gods, it shouldn't come as much of a surprise that we still can't get enough of them today. Kittens and cats are practically everywhere! Thanks to countless videos, gifs, and memes, they've won the Internet. Cats have also carved out their own space in the fashion sphere—couture companies, trusted fashion sites, and beloved bloggers have shown that it's okay for serious fashion to also have a sense of humor. It's not just the stereotypical cat ladies (and gents!) who have jumped onboard, though—it seems to be just about everyone, and the reason is simple: Cats make people happy! This book was created with that same spirit.

Our furry (and, yes, sometimes bald) cat friends supply us with an incredible amount of inspiration, and that translates into a *lot* of creativity, as reflected in the broad array of crafts in this book. The projects are divided into sections—accessories, fashion, home, and entertaining—all with an extensive range of skills, including sewing, patternmaking, appliqué, jewelry-making, and more. Some of the projects are a bit tongue-in-cheek (and there are more than a few cat puns), but this book is super serious about delivering clear, high-quality tutorials. From quirky and hip to sweet and subtle, the wide variety of DIYs in these pages ensures that everyone can find the purr-fect project!

Getting Started: Techniques, Tips & Materials

HAND-STITCHING TECHNIQUES

For the most part, the sewing in this book is done by hand, though there are some projects—such as the Persian Cat Wrap Skirt (page 37) or the "It's Meow or Never" Zip Case (page 7) or the Origami Shirt Pocket (page 46)—that can be done with a sewing machine. If you don't have a sewing machine, not to worry. You can get the same great results with hand sewing. Below is a list of basic stitches to use.

Running Stitch

Creating a Running Stitch couldn't be easier. Just go in and out through the materials while keeping even spacing in between each stitch.

Double Running Stitch

Double Running Stitch begins the same as Running Stitch, but when you get to the end of the row, reverse direction, sewing back through the exact same holes. This fills in the spaces between the first row of stitches, resulting in a line that resembles the look of a sewing machine.

Whip Stitch

The Whip Stitch is a simple, decorative stitch that is created in much the same way as a Running Stitch. The only difference is that you will be going over the edge, making the stitch from the back to the front each time.

Double Whip Stitch

The Double Whip Stitch is a continuation of a standard Whip Stitch. Just like with the Double Running Stitch, when you get to the end of your row, reverse directions, sewing another Whip Stitch until you reach the point where you began.

Split Stitch

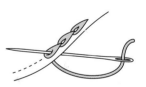

A Split Stitch is an embroidery technique for creating lines and outlines. Start by making a stitch in your fabric. Your next stitch will come up through the midpoint of the previous stitch. Continuing stitching one stitch into another to create a chain. This will be used for outlining on projects, such as the Kitty Cuff Bracelet (page 19).

Satin Stitch

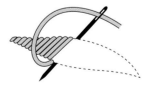

Satin Stitch is used to completely and smoothly fill in a shape with thread. Start by stitching, or drawing if you are using a template, your shape onto your material. Beginning on the left side, make a long, flat stitch followed by another directly next to it, a little longer or shorter as needed. The stitches should be placed side-by-side from the top of the design to the bottom. When you reach the right side, your design should be completely filled a smooth, raised grouping of parallel stitches.

Criss-Cross Stitch

Criss-Cross Stitch is very similar to a traditional Cross-stitch. Use an erasable fabric pen, pencil, or chalk to outline two parallel rows of dots. 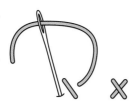 Starting with the bottom-left dot, bring the needle up through the fabric and stitch upward to the dot that's above and to the right. Your next stitch will come up through the bottom dot just beneath that top stitch. Repeat this process until you reach the right side. Now go from the bottom-left stitch up to the dot above and to the left. Repeat until you reach the left side. When you're finished, the stitches will look like Xs. To make a Double Criss-Cross Stitch, overlap two Criss-Cross Stitches at alternating angles.

Combination Stitches

Now that you know these basics, you can combine them for different looks. For example, layering a Double Running Stitch with a Double Whip Stitch as seen in the Feline Felt Storage Bin (page 55) not only gives a great look but also provides added strength to the edge!

WORKING WITH TEMPLATES

A lots of templates are used in this book. For best results, I suggest making a photocopy of the templates, so you can keep the original in pristine shape—this also allows you to easily make any of the projects more than once. This is particularly handy if you are having a craft night with your friends!

TRANSFERRING DESIGNS

For some projects, such as the C.R.E.A.M. Tote (page 12), you need to transfer a design onto your materials. There are a number of ways to do this. Below are three techniques. Use whichever seems to make the most sense for your specific project.

Carbon Paper

Place a piece of carbon paper face down on your material with the design placed faceup on top. Trace around the design, either with a pencil or a tracing wheel. I'd suggest trying this on a scrap piece of fabric first to get the hang of it before working directly on your materials. This will ensure that the markings are visible on the fabric and that you are only leaving markings exactly where you need them.

Light

Lay your material on top of the design template, and place both layers on a light box or against a brightly lit window. The light showing through should make your design visible enough to trace with an erasable fabric pen, pencil, or chalk.

Pinholes

Use an awl or straight pin to make a number of holes on the outlines of the design, piercing the paper. Place the template onto your fabric and color a dot over each of the holes with an erasable fabric pen, pencil, or chalk. When you pick up the paper, you will see the dots on the fabric indicating where your design will be.

PROTECT YOURSELF, PROTECT YOUR STUFF

Like most fun activities, crafting can sometimes get a bit messy. If your project involves glues, paints, or any kind of spray, it's best to make sure that you and your work areas are both covered. A simple smock and rubber gloves should take care of you, and butcher paper or old newspaper can safely cover your work surface—though be conscious of newsprint transferring onto fabrics. If you have a project that involves multiple colors of paint, I'd recommend keeping a few paper plates around for easy organizing and cleanup. And be sure that any projects using spray paint or spray adhesive are done outside, where there is proper ventilation.

YOU DO YOU

One of my favorite parts of cat imagery is how iconic it is. Even if there's nothing more than a circle with two triangles on top, it's unmistakable. You'll notice that some of the projects in this book are a subtle, minimal take on a cat's shape, while others are far more detailed. I think the best projects are the ones that are most personal to *you*, so if you feel like adding more rhinestones, more embroidery, or subtracting some—or all—of it, anything goes! This is all about what appeals most to your personal aesthetic.

MATERIALS

Fabric

If you've ever stepped into a fabric store, then you know there are tons of different fabrics in every weight, texture, and print imaginable. The fabric projects in this book don't require anything fancy, so feel free to grab a fabric that you are most drawn to. However, it's a good practice to have your future creation in mind when fabric shopping. For example, a stretchy fabric is probably not the best pairing for projects like the Origami Shirt Pocket (page 46) or the "It's Meow or Never" Makeup Zip Case (page 7), as they'll be less likely to hold their shape over time.

Leather, Vinyl, and Felt

The great thing about leather, vinyl, and felt is that when you cut them, they don't leave a frayed edge behind. Because of that, you may use these materials interchangeably for the projects in this book. However, be sure to take note that, just like fabric, these textiles can come in a variety of different weights and strengths. If you are substituting one of these materials for a project found in this book, make sure that you are using a material of similar quality.

A Word About Felt: You'll notice that a number of projects in this book use felt. Its affordability, vibrancy, and ease of use are just a few of the reasons why it's such a popular crafting material. However, be aware that not all felt is created equal. Some felt lacks in strength. Only one project in this book, the Feline Felt Storage Bin on page 55, requires strong felt. Other than that, your selected felt doesn't need to be the thickest or most expensive brand on the market, but just remember: quality matters. The better your felt, the nicer and more durable your finished project will be!

Cardstock

Cardstock is a bit thicker than regular paper, which gives it a little more strength. For any project in this book requiring cardstock, you are welcome to use a manila folder or an index card.

Embellishments

Lots of the projects in these pages use embellishments. My favorites are sequins, rhinestones, and other shiny beads. If these don't fit with your aesthetic, feel free to substitute an embellishment that is more to your taste. Going rogue is always encouraged!

Accessories

Sometimes a small piece can have a whole lot of impact.
These accessory projects are the perfect way to start adding
a liberal dose of cats to your day-to-day routine.

Bib Necklace

This big and bold necklace is the perfect finishing touch for your outfit and the ultimate standout accessory for cat lovers.

What You Need:

Template (page 91)

Pencil

Scissors

Leather (or vinyl or felt),
  7½ x 3½ inches (19 x 9 cm)

Hole punch, ⅛ inch (4 mm)
  wide

Awl

2 diamond-shaped rhinestones,
  approx. 1½ inches (4 cm)
  long, in green

Embroidery needle

Embroidery floss in green
  and pink

Ribbon, 2 pieces, each approx.
  ¼ inch x 1 foot (6 mm x 30 cm)
  long

What You Do:

1. Use the template to trace and cut out your piece of leather. For a reminder on working with templates and transferring designs, see page x.

2. Use the hole punch to create the two holes indicated on the template **(A)**.

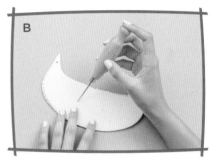

3. Place the template over your cut piece of leather. Position the rhinestones in the desired location, and draw dots to outline them. Do the same for the whiskers. Using the awl, pierce a hole at each dot **(B)**.

4. Use the needle and green embroidery thread to stitch the rhinestones onto the leather **(C)**, using the holes you made with the awl for placement. Then use the pink embroidery floss to stitch on the whiskers with a long Running Stitch.

5. Finish the necklace by inserting the ribbon into each of the ear holes and tying a knot on each end that is large enough to prevent the ribbon from slipping back through the hole **(D)**.

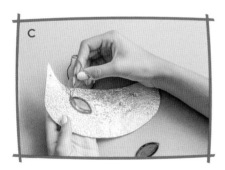
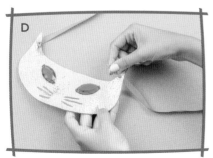

Cat Ring

A mini-version of the Bib Necklace, this playful ring may be
a lot smaller in scale but is no less catty!

What You Need:

Template (page 91)

Pencil

Scissors

Ruler

Leather (or vinyl or felt),
1 x 3 ½ inches (2.5 x 8.5 cm)

Awl

Sewing needle

Cotton thread, in turquoise

2 rhinestones, ⅜ inches (1 cm)
long, in turquoise

Embroidery needle

Embroidery floss in red

What You Do:

1. Photocopy or trace the template onto a sheet of paper
   and cut it out to create your pattern **(A)**. If you trace it,
   remember to transfer all of the dots as well.

   *Note: Keeping the original pattern in good shape is especially
   important for this project. Using a copy will allow you to
   make more in different sizes.*

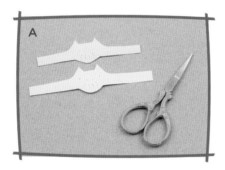

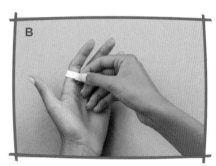

2. Wrap the pattern around your finger. Crease the paper where
   the pieces overlap **(B)**.

3. Use a ruler to add ¼ inch (6 mm) mark to either side of the
   creases **(C)**, and cut away excess **(D)**.

4. Now that the pattern is fitted to your finger, lay it on top of
   the leather, trace the pattern, and cut it out **(E)**.

5. Place the pattern on top of the cut leather and use the awl
   to pierce the leather at each of the dots **(F)**.

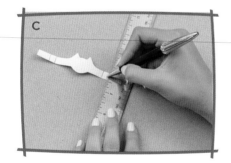

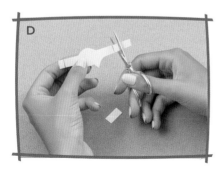

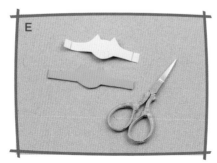

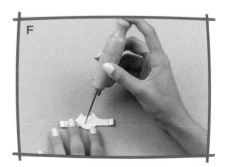

6. Using the sewing needle and cotton thread, stitch the rhinestones over the eyes **(G)**. Stitch the whiskers with the embroidery needle and embroidery floss **(H)**.

7. Wrap the leather into a ring shape, overlapping the edges by ¼ inch (6 mm), and stitch closed **(I)**.

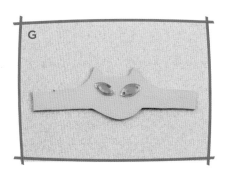

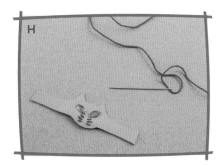

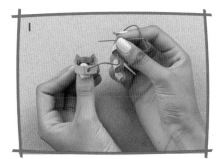

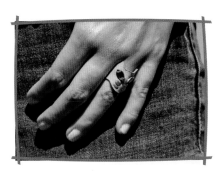

"It's Meow or Never" Makeup Zip Case

Upcycling the denim from an old pair of jeans can make good use of material. It can also give your finished zip case a beautiful (and authentic) worn-in look.

What You Need:

Denim, 1 pant leg from a worn-out pair of jeans or a piece of denim measuring 9½ x 15 inches (24 x 38 cm)

Iron

Zipper, 7 inches (17.5 cm) long

Iron-on letters, 1 inch (2.5 cm) tall, in color of your choice

Sewing needle (or sewing machine)

Sewing thread

Tassel in coordinating color (optional)

What You Do:

1. Cut two denim rectangles, each measuring 7 x 8¼ inches (17.5 x 21 cm), plus a strip measuring 1 x 3 inches (2.5 x 7.5 cm) **(A)**.

2. On both rectangles, fold back the top edge by ¼ inch (6 cm) and iron it down **(B)**.

3. On the strip, fold back one of the long sides by ¼ inch (6 cm) and iron it down.

4. Cut the strip in half widthwise so you have two pieces, each measuring 1½ inches (4 cm) long **(C)**.

5. Place a strip on each end of the zipper tape, right where the teeth stop. The fold should be facing in toward the zipper **(D)**.

6. Use sewing needle and thread (or a sewing machine) to stitch the strip onto the zipper tape along the folded edge **(E)**.

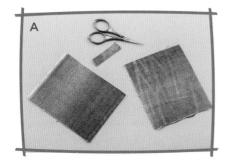

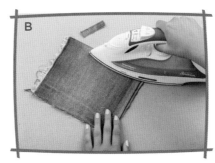

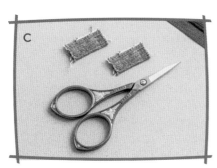

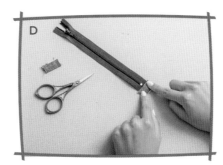

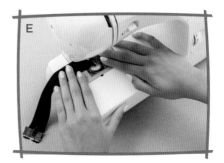

7. Place the folded edge of the denim rectangles on each of the zipper tape's long sides **(F)** and stitch all the way across along the fold **(G)**.

8. Fold the denim together so that the right sides are touching. When the edges are lined up, pin together **(H)**. Unzip the zipper about halfway.

9. Stitch all the way around the three sides ¼ inch (6 mm) from the edge **(I)**.

10. Flip right-side out **(J)**.

11. Collect and arrange the letters for the message on the case, and use scissors to cut out the apostrophe from one of the unused letters **(K)**.

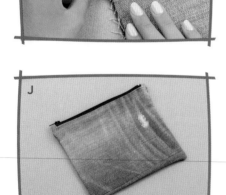

12. Use a ruler to help you line up your letters the way you want **(L)**, and then iron down **(M)**.

13. As an optional (but very pretty) finishing step, attach a tassel to the zipper pull **(N)**.

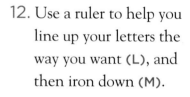

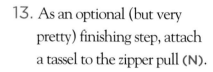

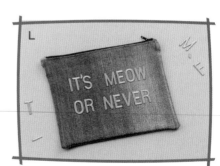

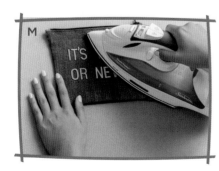

Hoop Earrings

Give a simple pair of hoop earrings a major style upgrade by adding your favorite decorative paper and some cat embellishments.

What You Need:

Pencil

Ruler

Scrap paper, slightly larger than the hoop earrings

Hoop earrings, 1½ inches (4 cm) in diameter

Scissors

Decorative paper, 5 x 6 inches (12.5 x 15 cm)

Glue stick

Acrylic paint, markers, or gel pens in coordinating colors

Craft glue (or glue gun)

2 rhinestones, ¼ inch (6 mm) wide, in black

What You Do:

1. Use the pencil and ruler to draw two straight, perpendicular lines on the piece of scrap paper **(A)**.

2. Lay one of the hoop earrings over the lines so that the top quarter of the hoop is above the horizontal line, with its midpoint (not including the part that goes through your ear) touching the vertical line **(B)**.

3. Trace around the portion of the hoop that's beneath the horizontal line, but only on the right side **(C)**.

4. Fold the paper in half along the vertical line.

5. Draw a little dip that extends from where the hoop drawing intersects the vertical line down toward the fold **(D)**.

6. Cut out. This will be your template **(E)**.

7. Trace the template onto the wrong side of your decorative paper twice **(F)**.

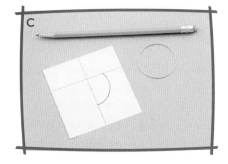

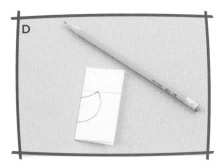

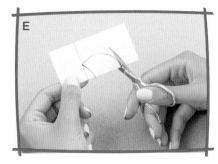

8. Cut both pieces out. Cut directly on the line at the dip, but leave at least ⅛ inch (3 mm) around the outside line (G).

9. Cover the wrong side of one of the papers with the glue stick and place your hoop directly over the outer tracing (H).

10. Cover the wrong side of the other paper with the glue stick. Carefully place it over top of the hoop, making sure that the dips on both are neatly lined up (I).

11. When you're happy with the placement, rub the surfaces firmly to help adhere the paper to the hoop (J).

12. Carefully cut all around the outside, close to the hoop, to remove the excess paper. Ideally, you still want a small amount of the front and back pieces touching outside of the hoop to add strength (K).

13. Repeat steps 7–12 to create the second earring in your pair.

14. Now the fun part! Use paint or markers to decorate each of the earrings with ears, whiskers, a nose, and eyes (L). Finish by gluing two rhinestones over the eyes (M).

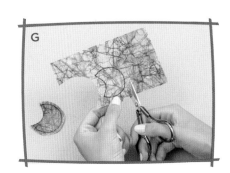

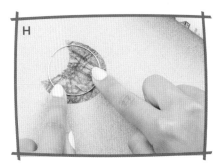

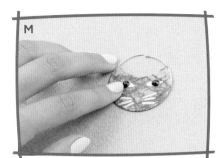

C.R.E.A.M. Tote

"Cats rule everything around me"—it's true! When your inspiration is one part feline and one part hip-hop, good crafting happens.

What You Need:

Template (page 92)

Erasable fabric pen, pencil, or chalk

Canvas tote bag

Fabric markers in black, purple, orange, blue, yellow, and green

What You Do:

1. Using the template and an erasable fabric pen, pencil, or chalk, transfer the design onto the front of your tote bag **(A)**. For a reminder on working with templates and transferring designs, see page x.

2. Color in the design as you like with fabric markers **(B, C)**.

Note: Be sure to read the instructions on your brand of fabric markers to find out how long they take to dry, or if heat-setting the ink with an iron is required.

Paw-some Phone Case

Because everyone's phone is different, this project starts by creating a custom pattern that's a purr-fect fit for *your* phone.

What You Need:

Pencil

2 sheets of paper

Ruler

Scissors

Thick felt, enough to wrap around your phone once with a little excess

Embroidery floss in white and pink

2 rhinestones, ¼ inch (6 mm), in turquoise blue

Embroidery needle

Glue gun

What You Do:

1. Trace the outline of your phone onto a sheet of paper **(A)**.

2. Measure the width of your phone **(B)**.

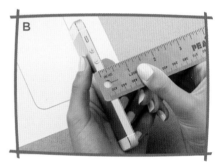

3. Add half of the width around the bottom and two sides of your tracing. Do not add anything to the top **(C)**.

4. Now add an additional ⅛ inch (3 mm) around the bottom and two sides **(D)**.

5. Cut this shape out, rounding the two bottom corners. This is the back of your pattern **(E)**.

6. Trace this shape onto the other sheet of paper, adding a convex curve at the top **(F)** that extends from the left corner to the right corner.

7. Cut this piece out to make the front of your pattern **(G)**.

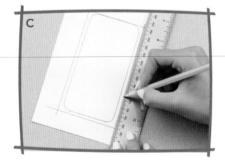
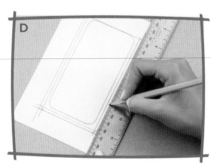

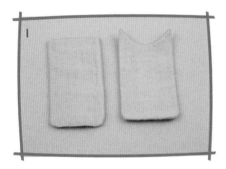

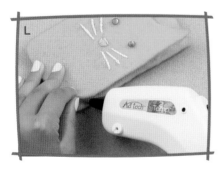

8. Trace both of the shapes onto your felt **(H)**, and cut them out **(I)**.

9. On the felt with the curve, use the embroidery needle and pink embroidery floss to Split Stitch a small inverted triangle at the center to form the outline of the cat's nose, and then fill it in with Satin Stitch. On both sides of the triangle, stitch three radiating 1-inch (2.5-cm) lines with the white embroidery floss using a Split Stitch to make whiskers, as shown **(J)**.

10. Glue the two rhinestones above the whiskers as shown **(K)**.

11. To finish, attach the two pieces of felt using the hot glue gun around the sides and bottom **(L)**. You only have a ⅛-inch (3-mm) allowance for gluing, so be very careful not to use more than this or it is likely to affect the fit of your phone case.

Note: Though you can make this project with any type of felt, selecting one on the thicker side will make for a nicer finished project while also giving your phone more protection.

Cat Wallet

Unfussy and fierce, this wallet is transformed with an iconic cat silhouette.

What You Need:

Templates (pages 94–95)

Stiff vinyl, 13 x 6 inches
(33 x 15 cm)

Pencil

Scissors

Awl

Transfer tape, ¼ inch (6 mm)
wide

Embroidery needle

Embroidery floss in pink
and white

What You Do:

1. Use the templates to trace the wallet shapes onto your vinyl, and cut out both shapes **(A)**. Transfer all of the indicated marks with an awl. For a reminder on working with templates and transferring designs, see page x.

2. On template A, cut the two ear lines **(B)**. This piece will serve as the wallet's flap.

 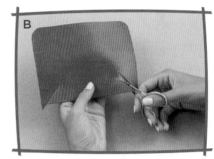

3. Place the transfer tape onto each of the cut pieces of vinyl in the areas shown **(C)**. (Like leather, vinyl will show pin holes, so pieces are best attached using transfer tape.) Be sure to place the tape only at the very edges. You don't want the interior of your wallet to be sticky!

4. Remove the backing from the tape on the backside of the flap piece and place it on the top edge of the larger piece **(D)**.

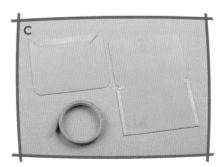 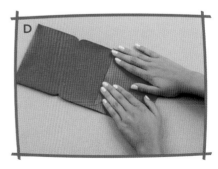

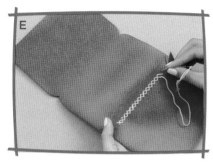

5. Stitch these pieces together using Criss-Cross Stitches **(E)**.

6. Remove the last of the transfer-tape backing and fold upward **(F)**. Double check that the two sides are perfectly lined up; if not, adjust accordingly.

7. Stitch the two sides with a Double Whip Stitch **(G)**. Continue Double Whip Stitch around the flap and ears **(H)**.

Note: By enlarging the templates on a copier, you can easily turn this project from wallet-size to clutch-size!

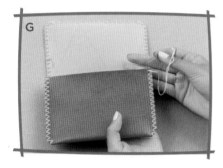

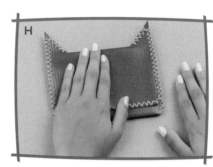

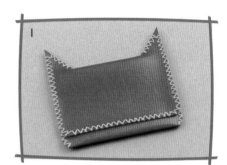

Kitty Cuff Bracelet

Created in the style of a formal shirt cuff, each of these bracelets makes one half of a cat's face. If you'd like to make a complete cat's face, flip the patterns for the second cuff so you'll have the full face when you hold your wrists together.

Tip: All of the decorative stitches in this project will employ an embroidery technique called a Split Stitch. If you're unsure how to do this, see page ix.

What You Need:

Pencil

Scissors

Templates (page 93)

Medium-weight cotton fabric, 4 x 10 inches (10 x 25 cm), in white

Satin fabric, 1 x 2 inches (2.5 x 5 cm), in both red and light aqua

Iron

Interfacing, 2 x 4 inches (5 x 10 cm)

Spray starch (if needed)

Embroidery floss in black

Embroidery needle

Hook-and-loop tape

Sewing needle (or sewing machine)

Sewing thread in white

Note: This makes one cuff, so double your materials and repeat the instructions to make two.

What You Do:

(Makes one cuff)

1. Use the templates to cut out all of the pieces of material that you'll need: two cuffs in the medium-weight white fabric **(A)** (to create the front and back); one circle from the aqua fabric; and one ear in the red fabric **(B)**. For a reminder on working with templates and transferring designs, see page x.

   Note: You do not need to cut out any pieces of fabric with the eye-shaped template. It is used for placement only.

2. Iron interfacing behind the aqua and red pieces. Trim away any excess interfacing.

3. Fold back ⅜ inch (1 cm) on all sides of the white fabric, and iron **(C)**. You may also stiffen it up with a little spray starch in this step if needed.

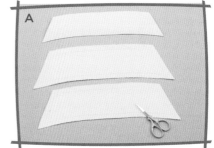

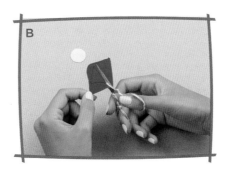

4. On one of the white pieces of fabric, decide on the placement you like for the ear, then use the black embroidery floss and an embroidery needle to stitch all around with a Split Stitch (D).

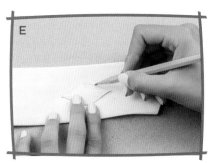

5. Now, trace the eye-shaped template with a pencil below and to the side of the stitched ear, as shown (E).

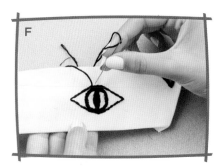

6. Place the aqua circle in the middle of the tracing and stitch all around the circle with a Split Stitch. Finish the eye by embroidering with a Split Stitch directly on the pencil marks. When you've finished, it should appear as shown (F).

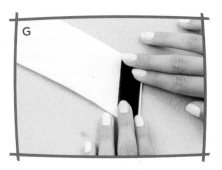

7. On the right side of the white fabric *without* the embroidered eye and ear, sew the hook-and-loop tape to the left and right sides as shown using the sewing needle and thread (G).

8. Put the wrong sides of the two pieces of white fabric together and sew around the perimeter (H).

Paw Print Sneakers

Make tracks in these glittery paw print shoes!

What You Need:

Pen

Scissors

Template (page 96)

Sheet of iron-on vinyl,
　5 x 7 inches (12.5 x 18 cm)

Canvas sneakers

Iron

Piece of scrap fabric,
　4 x 5 inches (10 x 12.5 cm)

What You Do:

1. Use the template to trace the paw print shape onto the sheet of iron-on vinyl. Trace and cut out at least 20 copies **(A)**, as each shoe will likely take 10 or more paw prints, depending upon your shoe size. For a reminder on working with templates and transferring designs, see page x.

2. Arrange the paw print shapes on the sneakers as shown **(B)**.

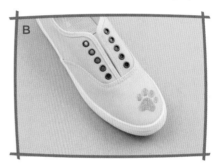

3. When you are happy with the placement, gently cover with a piece of fabric and press with the iron to secure **(C)**.

4. Pick up the fabric and check to see that all areas of the vinyl are fully ironed down. If not, repeat step 3.

   Note: This project can be done with any iron, but I recommend using a mini iron. You'll find it much easier to maneuver.

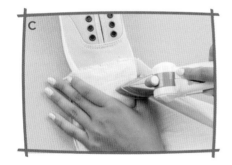

5. Repeat steps 2–4 until you are happy with the amount of paws covering the sneakers **(D)**.

   Note: It can be super cute to have a partial paw print in the areas close to the sole. To create this effect, arrange paw prints how you'd like them, then iron all the way up to the edge of the sole but not on the sole. The heat from the iron can easily mar the rubber soles, so you'll want to do your best to keep from touching the iron to them. When you lift the fabric off, use scissors to trim away the parts of the vinyl that overlapped the sole.

Decoupage Bengal Bangles

A whole lot of cats make this one great bracelet. Feel free to cut images from magazines or make this piece more personal by printing out pictures of your own sweet kitties.

What You Need:

Scissors

Images of cats (enough to create a collage atop the surface of your bangle)

Decoupage medium

Paintbrush

Plastic or wooden bangle

What You Do:

1. Cut out the shapes of the cats (A).

2. Use the decoupage medium and a paintbrush to glue the images to the bangle (B).

3. When the bangle is covered the way that you like, brush on a final coat of decoupage medium and allow it to dry (C).

Fashion

These apparel-focused projects let you bring along your feline friends wherever you go. At work, school, or out and about, these cats will bring a cheerful touch to your wardrobe.

Thigh-High Socks

Make this small alteration to your favorite pair of stockings
and give them some major cat-titude.

What You Need:

Template (page 96)

Pencil

Scissors

Felt, 3 x 5 inches
(7.5 x 12.5 cm), in black,
white, pink, and green

Cardboard

Thigh-high socks

Sewing thread in black

Sewing needle

Fabric glue

What You Do:

1. Use the template to trace **(A)** and cut out the all of the cat's
   features **(B)** from the felt as follows:
   - 4 ears in black felt
   - 4 eyes in green felt
   - 4 whiskers in white felt
   - 2 heart noses in pink felt

2. Place a piece of cardboard into the top of each sock. The
   cardboard should be 1½ inches (4 cm) wider than the top of
   the sock when unstretched **(C)**.

3. Insert the bottom portion of an ear ½ inch (12 mm) into the
   top of your thigh-high socks and stitch down with sewing
   thread and needle, as pictured **(D)**.

4. Glue the rest of the features to the sock with the fabric glue **(E)**.

5. Allow the glue enough time to dry completely before wearing.

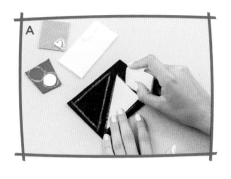

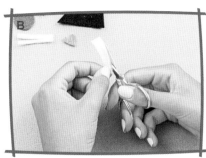

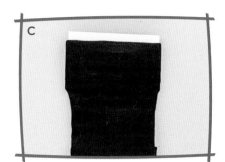

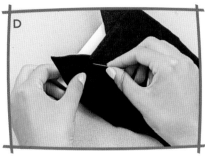

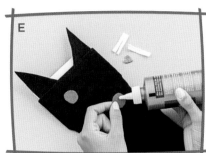

Elbow Patches

This done-in-a-hurry project is a modern take on traditional oval elbow patches. Ditch the standard ovals for this cat silhouette, and iron onto any top you please.

What You Need:

Pencil

Template (page 96)

Scissors

Iron-on elbow patches

Erasable fabric pen, pencil, or chalk

Iron

What You Do:

1. Trace the template onto two iron-on elbow patches **(A)** and carefully cut out **(B)**. For a reminder on working with templates and transferring designs, see page x.

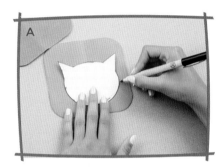

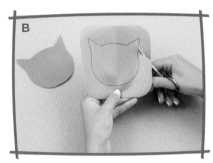

2. Put on the shirt and, using the erasable fabric pen, pencil, or chalk, make a small mark over each of your elbows **(C)**. Take off the shirt.

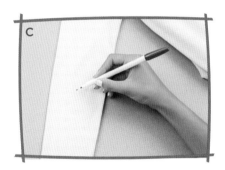

3. Place a patch over each of the elbow marks **(D)**.

4. Adjust as needed to make sure the patches are symmetrically aligned, then iron on. **(E)**

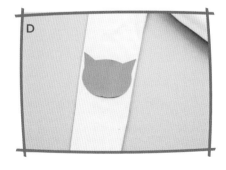

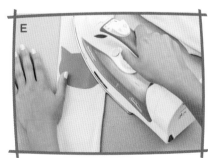

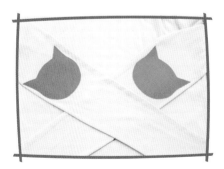

"Look at Me Meow" Bejeweled Collar

Bring some feline finesse to a collared work shirt with the addition of sequin and bead embellishments.

What You Need:

Shirt with a collar

Tracing paper

Pencil

Template (page 96)

Awl

Erasable fabric pen, pencil, or chalk

Sequins, as many as 40

Sewing needle

Sewing thread

8 long, thin beads, ⅜ inch (1 cm) long, metallic silver

Transfer tape (optional)

What You Do:

1. Lay the shirt's collar out flat with the right side facing up **(A)**.

2. Cover that portion of the collar with a piece of tracing paper and trace all around with a pencil **(B)**.

3. Place the traced collar flat on a work surface, and place the template under this tracing until you are happy with the positioning of the image on the collar. Pierce each dot on the template with an awl **(C)**.

Note: If your collar is much bigger or smaller than the template, shrink or increase the size on a copier machine until it's a size that works for your specific shirt collar.

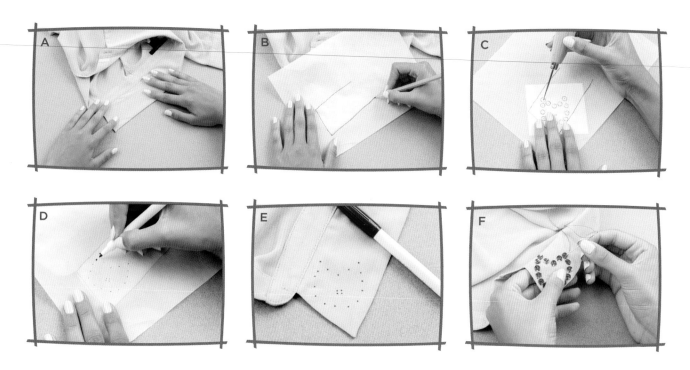

4. Transfer the dots on the template to one side of the collar using the erasable fabric pen, or pencil **(D, E)**. For a reminder on working with templates and transferring designs, see page x.

5. Place the tracing paper on top of the collar's opposite end, and repeat step 4.

6. Now you're ready to begin sewing on the sequins! Position a sequin directly over a dot and sew it on with needle and thread. When you're sure it's secured, knot the remaining string and cut. This makes the overall design much more durable. (Optional: To hold a sequin steady while you sew, put a small piece of transfer tape beneath it and tape it down before sewing.) Repeat until all of the sequins have been sewn into place **(F)**.

7. Finish by sewing the four long beads at each cat head's center to create "whiskers" **(G)**.

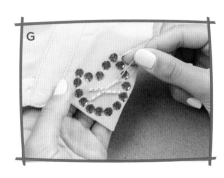

Pom-Pom Tank

With just a couple of strategic snips and a little bit of sewing, a handful
of pom-poms can be transformed into a herd of cats.

What You Need:

Knit top

Lots of pom-poms, 1 inch
(2.5 cm) wide

Scissors

Embroidery thread in black,
white, and at least one more
color of your choice

Sewing needle

Sewing thread

*Note: This project works
best on knit tops—the sturdier
the better. You can also use
this technique on your winter
wardrobe to dress up a drab
sweater!*

What You Do:

1. Make all of the pom-poms "cat shaped." To do this, squeeze
one pom-pom between your fingers until it is somewhat
flattened. While maintaining this flattened shape between
your fingers, carefully cut a small wedge shape from it **(A)**.
(You will want the wedge to be close to the center, but not
completely cut to the center **(B)**, as this is the area that holds
all of the pom-pom's strands together.)

   *Note: It may take a couple of tries to get the
   pom-poms to look the way you'd like, but don't give up!
   Once you get the hang of it, it's super easy.*

2. Repeat step 1 until you have enough pom-poms to adorn
your top.

3. Create the cat features for the pom-poms. Start by sewing the
whiskers in an "X" shape on the bottom half of the pom-pom
using any of the colors except white or black **(C)**.

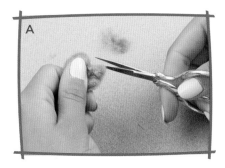

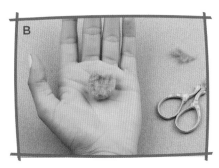

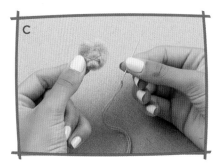

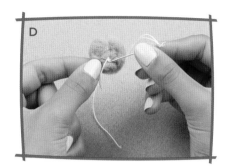

4. Add a nose with one or two small Running Stitches in white embroidery thread across the center of the "X" **(D)**.

5. Finish by adding two eyes in black embroidery thread, positioned just above the "X" **(E)**. Sometimes the eyes can get lost in the pom-pom fluff; stitch over the same spot a couple of times to make them more visible, if needed.

6. Repeat steps 3–5 on remaining pom-poms **(F)**.

7. Decide how you'd like to arrange the pom-poms on your top and finish by stitching them all to the fabric using the sewing needle and thread **(G)**. Each stitch should go left to right or from top to bottom at the midpoint of the pom-poms to keep the stitches from being visible.

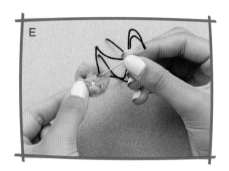

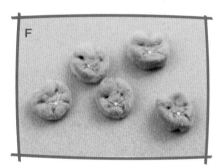

Persian Cat Wrap Skirt

There is nothing subtle about this skirt! It's furry, full of fun,
charm, and custom-made to fit you.

What You Need:

Flexible tape measure

Pencil and paper

Two sheets of newspaper or
large pattern paper

Ruler

Pencil

Scissors

Faux fur, at least 1 yard (91 cm)

Erasable fabric pen

2 pieces of waistband elastic,
each 1 inch (2.5 cm) long

2 buttons, ¾ inch (2 cm) in
diameter

Templates (page 98)

Felt, 4 x 8 inches (10 x 20 cm),
in blue

Felt, 6 x 8 inches (15 x 20 cm),
in black

Felt, 8 x 10 inches (20 x 25.5 cm),
in white

Felt, 4 x 4 inches (10 x 10 cm),
in pink

Sewing needle (or sewing
machine)

Sewing thread in same color as
faux fur

Embroidery needle

Embroidery thread in black,
pink, and white

What You Do:

1. Using the flexible measuring
   tape, measure the
   circumference of your waist
   at the point where you want
   the skirt to sit (A). Record
   this measurement and
   label it "A." Measure from your waist to wherever you want
   the skirt to end—thigh, knee, etc.—and then add two inches
   (5 cm). This number will determine the length of your skirt,
   including room for the top and bottom seam allowances.
   Record this measurement and label it "B."

Create the A-Line Skirt Templates:

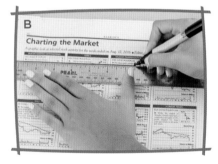

2. Fold one of the sheets of
   newspaper or pattern paper
   in half, and use a ruler to
   draw a horizontal line out
   from the fold that is ¼ of
   measurement "A" (B).

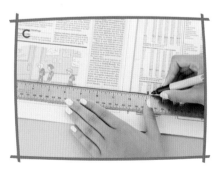

3. Measuring along the
   paper's fold, measure "B"
   inches down from that
   line to mark your desired
   skirt length. Draw a
   perpendicular line out from
   that mark to indicate the
   bottom hemline of your
   skirt (C).

*Note: The length you draw this line is up to you—the longer
it is, the wider your A-line skirt will be.*

4. Connect the ends of the top edge and bottom hemline (D).

5. Keeping the paper folded in half, cut out the shape (E).

6. Open it up and write "Pattern A" on it (F).

7. Place Pattern A on top of a second sheet of pattern paper or newspaper and trace it. Use a ruler to add 1 inch (2.5 cm) to the left and right sides—these are seam allowances (G).

8. Cut this shape out and label it "Pattern B" (H).

Cut the Fabric and Assemble the Skirt:

9. Place each pattern on the wrong side of your faux fur. You will need two pieces of Pattern A (I) and one piece of Pattern B (J). Trace the patterns onto the fabric using the erasable fabric pen, then cut out each piece.

10. With right sides together, line up the edge of one Pattern A piece of fabric with the right-hand edge of the Pattern B piece of fabric, and pin together.

11. With right sides together, line up the edge of the second Pattern A piece of fabric with the left-hand edge of the Pattern B piece of fabric, and pin together.

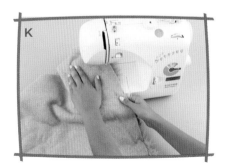

12. Stitch both edges, leaving a 1-inch (2.5 cm) seam allowance (K).

13. Now fold the top edge in 1 inch (2.5 cm), wrong sides together, and stitch down. Repeat on the bottom hemline.

Add the Closures:

14. Fold one of the pieces of elastic in half to form a loop. On the wrong side of the fur, sew the loop onto the top right corner. 1 inch (2.5 cm) away from the right-hand edge of the skirt (L).

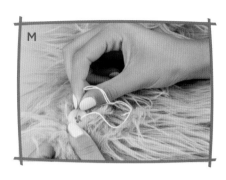

15. Stitch one of the buttons onto the right side of the fur, 1 inch (2.5 cm) away from the left-hand edge of the skirt (M).

16. Wrap the skirt around yourself, keeping the top edge in line with itself. On the wrong side of the fur, places pins (or binder clips) to mark the spots where the fabric overlaps the piece of elastic and the button (N).

17. Take off the skirt. In the spot pinned beneath the elastic, sew a button. In the spot pinned beneath the button, sew an elastic loop (O).

Add the Embellishments:

18. Now that the skirt has been assembled, use the templates on page 98 to trace and cut out the pieces of felt (P). Use the templates to cut out all of your felt pieces as follows:

- 2 template A shapes in black
- 2 template B shapes in blue
- 4 template C shapes in white
- 1 template D shape in pink
- 6 template E shapes in white

For a reminder on working with templates and transferring designs, see page x.

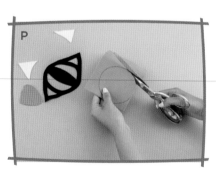

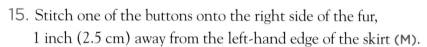

19. Assemble each eye by using the black embroidery thread to sew the blue felt to the back of the black felt, followed by the white pieces **(Q)**.

20. Find the placement that you like for the eyes, nose, and mouth, and stitch them onto the skirt with Running Stitch using coordinating embroidery thread **(R)**.

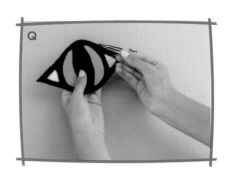

Embroidered Jeans

Inspired by sashiko embroidery, this simple embellishment
can add novelty to an old pair of jeans.

What You Need

Pencil

Scissors

Template (page 97)

Awl

Jeans

2 skeins embroidery floss
  in white

Embroidery needle

Erasable fabric pen (not pencil
  or chalk)

What You Do:

1. Photocopy or trace the
   template onto a sheet of
   paper and cut it out to
   create your pattern. Pierce
   each dot on the design
   with the awl (A).

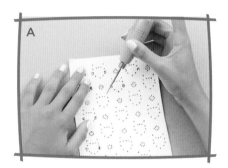

2. Decide where you would like the design to appear on the
   jeans, lay the template over this area, and use the erasable
   fabric pen to transfer the design by making a dot through
   each hole (B, C). Work on a flat surface or pin the paper to
   the fabric to keep the template stationary over the jeans.
   For a reminder on working with templates and transferring
   designs, see page x.

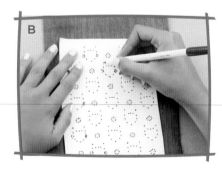

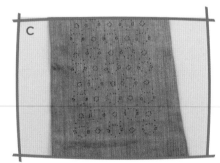

3. Starting with the cluster
   of dots at the top left-hand
   side, make the star design.
   Do this with Double Criss-
   Cross Stitch by stitching
   from the top-middle point in
   the design down to the point
   directly across from it (D).

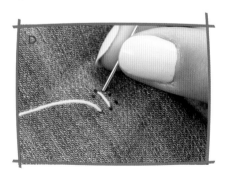

4. Move clockwise to the next point, and stitch to the point across from it (E).

5. Repeat step 4 until the star is complete, then move on to the cat head to its right (F).

6. To stitch the cat heads, start with the dot at the center-top point. With a Running Stitch, stitch around the shape in a clockwise direction until you are once again at the center-top point.

7. Now reverse direction (G), sewing counterclockwise to fill in the design with Double Running Stitch. As you get to the dots for the three whiskers, stitch them in (H).

8. Continue stitching each row of cats and stars, from left to right, until everything is completely filled in (I).

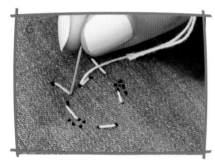

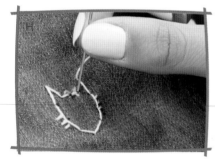

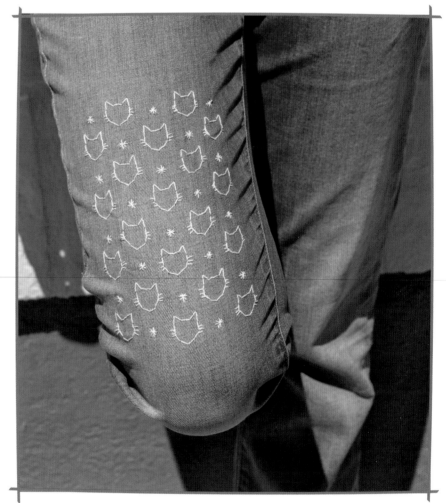

Cat-titude Cat Mask

Perfect for Halloween, or one of those days when you just need a disguise.

What You Need:

Templates (page 99)

Pencil

Scissors

Ribbon, 1 yard (91 cm) long, ½ inch wide (12 mm)

Craft foam, 4 x 9 inches (10 x 23 cm), in glittery black

Craft foam, 2 x 4 inches (5 x 10 cm), in white

Felt, 1 x 1¼ inches (2.5 x 3 cm), in pink

Cardstock, 1 x 1¼ inches (2.5 x 3 cm)

Glue gun

What You Do:

1. Using the templates, trace the mask onto the glittery black craft foam and the nose onto the pink felt and cardstock **(A)**. For a reminder on working with templates and transferring designs, see page x. Cut out all of the pieces, including the area for the eyes. Cut 6 whiskers, each ⅛ x 3½ inches, from white craft foam.

2. Glue three whiskers on each half of the cardstock nose **(B)**, then glue the felt nose onto the "unwhiskered" side of the cardstock **(C)**.

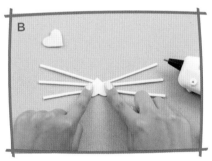

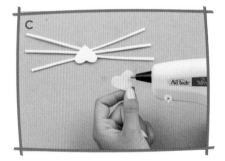

3. Glue the whiskered side of the cardstock down to the tab on the center front of the mask as shown **(D)**.

4. Cut your ribbon in half and glue the two pieces to either side of the mask to be used as ties **(E)**. Shorten as needed.

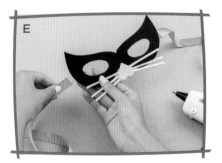

Origami Shirt Pocket

This project may be small, but it makes for a big improvement on an otherwise plain shirt.

What You Need:

Pencil

Ruler

Non-stretch fabric, at least 8½ x 8½ inches (21.5 x 21.5 cm)

Scissors

Spray starch

Iron

Shirt

Sewing needle (or sewing machine)

Sewing thread in color to match non-stretch fabric

Straight pins

Note: The more precisely you line up your edges at every step of the ironing, the better your overall project will be!

What You Do:

1. Begin by marking a square 8½ x 8½ inches (21.5 x 21.5 cm) on your fabric and cutting it out **(A)**.

2. On the backside of the fabric square, draw a line on each of the sides ½ inch (12 mm) from the edge **(B)**.

3. Give the fabric a spray of starch, then fold each edge on the lines and iron flat **(C)**.

4. Fold in half diagonally with wrong sides together and iron flat **(D)**.

5. Follow the illustrated steps, ironing after each of the folds **(E, F, G, H)**. Spray the fabric with the starch as you work, if needed.

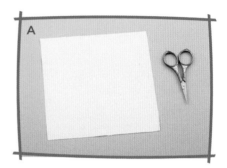

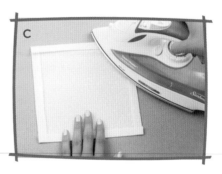

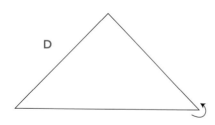

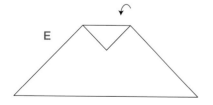

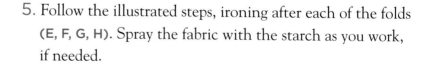

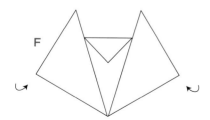

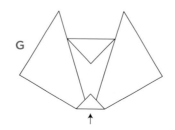

6. Topstitch the inner portion on both ears, and then sew the top portion of the cat's head (I).

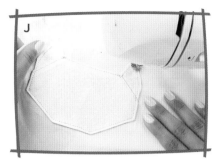

7. Pin the pocket onto your preferred area of the shirt.

8. Securely Topstitch from the top-outer point of the left ear, down and around the bottom of the head, and back up until you get to the top of the right ear (J). You could also use a Double-Running Stitch if you're sewing by hand.

Note: If you're topstitching using a sewing machine, experiment with stitch settings on a similar piece of fabric as your shirt, and choose the stitch length that best complements your fabric.

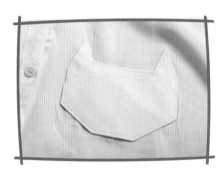

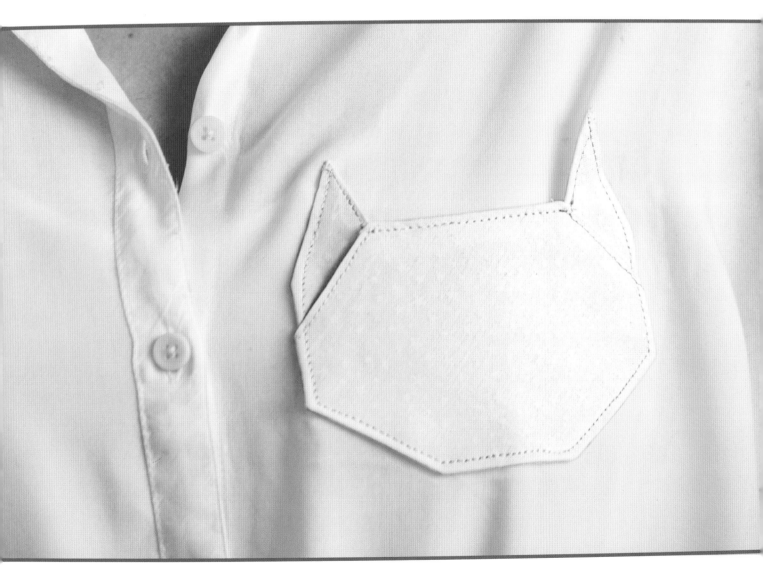

Home

Every house feels more like a home when there are cats around!
These new, no-maintenance friends are sure to make every room in
your house feel cozier and a whole lot more cheerful.

Paw Print Stamp

Leave your mark with this upcycled stamping project!

What You Need:

Empty thread spool

Pencil

Index card, large enough
to cover the top of your
thread spool

Scissors

Glue

Template (page 99)

Craft foam, 2 x 2 inches
(5 x 5 cm)

Ink pad

What You Do:

1. Prepare your spool: Trace one end of the spool onto an index card and cut out the circle **(A)**.

2. Glue the circle to the bottom of the spool **(B)**. Allow to dry.

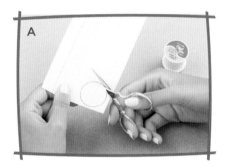

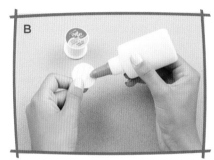

3. Trace the template patterns onto the craft foam and carefully cut them out **(C)**. For a reminder on working with templates and transferring designs, see page x.

4. Glue each craft-foam piece onto the index card–covered end of the spool in the same arrangement as pictured **(D)**. Allow to dry completely.

5. Once it's dry, your stamp is ready! Press the craft-foam end of the spool onto an ink pad and then apply to surfaces with even pressure **(E)**.

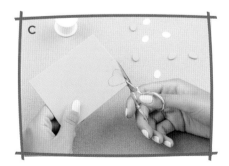

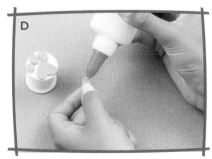

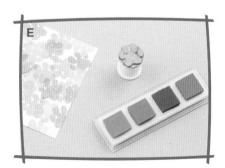

6. When you've finished using it, clean the surface by repeatedly pressing it onto a piece of scrap paper until it no longer leaves an image.

Su-purr-ior Stationery

Add some feline friendliness to your snail mail!

What You Need:

Pencil

Templates (page 99)

Circle-shaped stationery, 5¾ inches (14.5 cm) in diameter or cardstock that is at least 6 x 6 inches (15 x 15 cm)

Awl

Scissors

Ruler

Glue stick

Origami papers

Envelopes, 5¾ x 5¾ inches (14.5 x 14.5 cm) (optional)

What You Do:

1. Trace the template onto your round stationery **(A)** and transfer all of the indicated marks with an awl **(B)**. Alternatively, trace the template and indicated marks onto cardstock and cut the shape out. For a reminder on working with templates and transferring designs, see page x.

2. Cut out the shape at the top of the card **(C)**.

3. Use a ruler and pencil to draw a line across the card connecting the two awl marks.

4. Spread glue on the top 2 inches (5 cm) of the card, above the pencil line **(D)**.

5. Lay origami paper right-side up over the card, lining it up with the pencil line **(E)**.

6. Rub well to make sure the paper adheres.

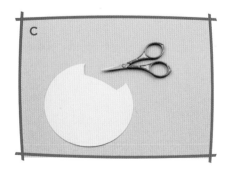  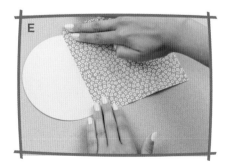

7. Flip over the card so you can see the excess origami paper, and carefully cut it away **(F)**.

8. Repeat steps 1–7 until you've created a colorful set of stationery.

Optional: If you would like to continue the cat theme onto the envelopes, trace the asterisk template (recognized as the infamous cat butt!) onto some to the scraps of origami paper **(G)**.
* *After you've sealed the envelope with the letter inside, glue the asterisk over the flap* **(H)**. *It should give someone a laugh once they realize what it is!*

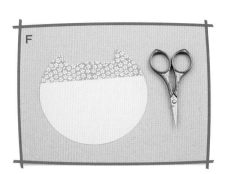

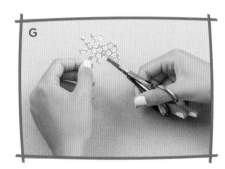

Feline Felt Storage Bin

Make your organizing more fun with one of these subtly catty storage bins.

What You Need:

Tailor's chalk

Templates (pages 100–101)

Felt, at least ¼ inch (6 mm) thick, 8 x 32 inches (20 x 81 cm), in gray

Scissors

Ruler

Transfer tape, ¼ inch (6 mm) wide (or 9 binder clips)

Felt, at least ¼ inch (6 mm) thick, 1 x 10 inches (2.5 x 25.5 cm), in black or a contrasting color

Embroidery thread in black or to match the contrasting color

Embroidery needle

Glue gun (optional)

What You Do:

1. Use the tailor's chalk to trace all templates onto the gray felt, and cut out the pieces (A). For a reminder on working with templates, see page x.

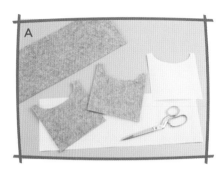

Note: To make a bigger or smaller storage bin, simply enlarge or shrink the templates as needed on a copier.

2. On the rectangular felt piece, use a ruler and tailor's chalk to draw a straight line ¼ inch (6 mm) from the edge on the long right and left sides (B).

3. On the square pieces, do the same to each of the three sides *without* the curved edge (C).

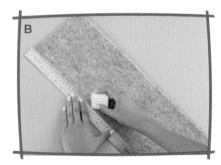

4. Run transfer tape or attach binder clips on the edge along the three sides as pictured (D).

5. Remove the tape's backing and apply it to the left side of the long piece. Make sure all of the edges are perfectly aligned.

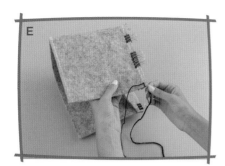

6. Starting from the top-left edge, sew these two pieces together using the embroidery thread and needle with a Double Running Stitch. Sew directly onto the lines from the tailor's chalk to properly align your stitches **(E)**.

7. When you've finished the Double Running Stitch, it will look like the picture to the left **(F)**.

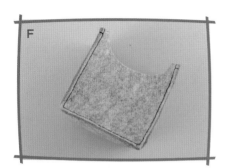

8. You may stop here, but if you'd like to add a bit more of a decorative flare, run a Double Whip Stitch over this same edge. This will also give the edges added strength **(G)**.

9. Repeat steps 3 through 6 on the other side.

10. When you're finished, cut two strips of felt in the contrast color measuring ⅜ x 12 inches (1 x 30 cm) **(H)**.

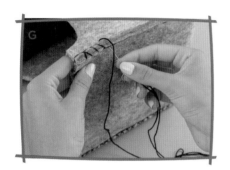

11. Line up the ends of the two pieces, then tie a knot in the middle **(I)**. These are the whiskers. Trim the ends if needed.

12. Attach the whiskers to one of the box's curved-top sides by stitching them down or with a glue gun **(J)**.

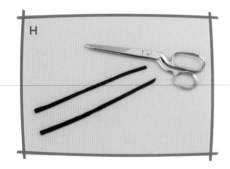

Cat Magnets

This frisky magnet set will help you keep track of your shopping lists. They are so fun to make, and it takes less than ten minutes to create a whole assortment.

What You Need:

Glue gun

Small magnet (the stronger the better)

Plastic cat figurine, approximately 2 inches (5 cm) tall

Spray paint in color of your choice

What You Do:

1. Place a drop of hot glue onto the back of the plastic cat figurine (A).

2. Place the magnet onto the glue and press firmly to adhere (B).

3. Spray with two light coats of spray paint. Allow to dry completely before using (C).

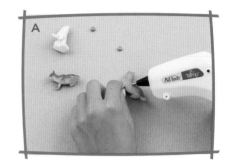

Kitty-Cat Wreath

Adorn your door with this super pretty wreath with a catty twist.

What You Need:

Wired twine, 4 feet (1.2 m)

Artificial greenery garland, 6 feet (1.8 m) in length

Florist's wire

Scissors

Various artificial flowers

Glue gun

What You Do:

1. Begin bending the wired twine so that it is a rounded shape approximately 12 inches (30.5 cm) in diameter. Wrap additional wired twine around the shape to give the wreath's foundation more strength. Twist the ends into the wired twine to close the circle (A).

2. Using the photo as a guide, bend the top of the shape to create points on the right and left sides for ears. It should resemble a cat's head (B).

3. Begin wrapping the greenery around the shape as many times as you'd like until the twine is no longer visible (C).

4. Wrap small pieces of florist's wire discreetly around both the twine and the greenery to reinforce their attachment (D).

5. Cut the stems off of the flowers, and arrange flowers on wreath as desired (E, F).

6. Finish by gluing the flowers into place with glue gun (G).

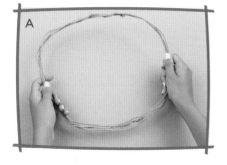

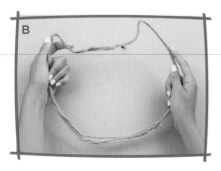

Cat's Meow Coasters

Fuse beads are a ubiquitous craft supply enjoyed by kids and adults alike. They are used as building blocks for projects, often involving more than one hundred beads in many colors, placed in patterns or to create an image. The beads are then "fused" with heat, usually from an iron. In this project they go from merely decorative to highly functional cat coasters for entertaining friends—or just yourself.

What You Need:

Fuse beads, in your choice of colors

- face: 266 beads
- ears: 12 beads
- eyes: 16 beads
- whiskers: 22 beads
- nose: 4 beads
- mouth: 11 beads

Fuse bead grid

Template (page 102)

Iron

Parchment paper

Adhesive felt or foam

What You Do:

1. Place the fuse beads on the grid as shown on template (A). Preheat the iron to a medium setting.

2. Place the parchment paper over your design and iron (B). The beads on this side should be ironed well enough that they now appear more like squares than little circles.

3. Remove the paper and flip the coaster over, removing the grid.

4. Place the parchment paper over this side. Apply the iron, but this time use lighter pressure so that the beads are attached but still remain in a round shape (C).

5. On the adhesive paper on the backside of your felt, trace around the cat with a marker (D).

6. Use scissors to cut out the shape (E).

7. Remove the adhesive paper from the back of the felt and place down on the side with the more square-shaped beads (F).

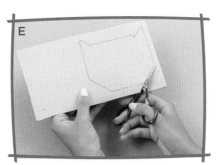

Cat Nap Throw Pillow

With this project, you can add a comfortable new companion
to your weekend binge-watching.

What You Need:

Templates (pages 104–105)

Pencil

Scissors

Felt, 5 x 6 inches (13 x 15 cm),
in green

Felt, 5 x 6 inches (13 x 15 cm),
in light blue

Felt, 4½ x 8½ inches
(11.5 x 21.5 cm), in turquoise

Felt, 13 x 14 inches
(33 x 35.5 cm), in black

Embroidery needle

Embroidery floss in black,
green and turquoise

Straight pins

Sewing needle

Sewing thread in black

Polyester fiberfill

Glue gun

2 rhinestones, ¼ inch (6 mm)
wide, in coordinating colors

Flat-back pearl
embellishments, ¼ inch
(6 mm) wide

What You Do:

1. Use the templates to cut out all of your felt pieces as follows **(A)**:
   - 7 small triangles in green
   - 7 large triangles in light blue
   - 2 ears in light blue
   - 2 eyes in turquoise
   - 1 nose in green
   - 1 belly in turquoise
   - 2 paws in light blue
   - 1 tail in black
   - 2 cat bodies in black

   For a reminder on working with templates and transferring
   designs, see page x.

2. Set aside one of the cat body pieces. On the other body
   piece, arrange the felt features. Be sure that the tail and the
   two paws overlap the belly **(B)**.

3. Stitch all of the felt features
   onto the front piece of
   the cat body using the
   embroidery needle and
   black floss with a Running
   Stitch **(C)**. When stitching
   the tail, switch to the green
   embroidery floss **(D)**.

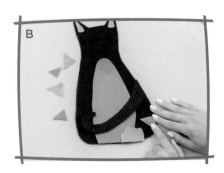

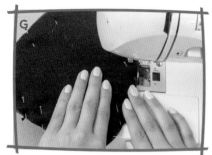

4. Stitch on the whiskers using turquoise floss with a Double Running Stitch.

5. Place the right sides of the cat body pieces together, and pin around the edges using the straight pins (E, F).

6. Using the sewing needle and sewing thread, stitch all around, ¼ inch (6 mm) from the edge, with a Double Running Stitch, leaving 3 inches (7.5 cm) unstitched at the bottom of the pillow (G). (You may choose to do this step on a sewing machine.)

7. Flip the felt right-side out (H).

8. Stuff the pillow with polyester fiberfill (I), then fold ¼ inch (6 mm) of the felt inward and stitch the open bottom closed with a Double Running Stitch (J).

9. Use a glue gun to attach the eyes, nose, and the pearl and rhinestone embellishments as shown (K).

Cat-cramé Planter

Upcycle some empty plastic containers into the purr-fect macramé planter that's fit to be tied.

What You Need:

Plastic container (cleaned and emptied) at least 3 inches (7.5 cm) wide

Permanent marker

Ruler

Rubber band (optional)

Kitchen or household shears (capable of cutting through plastic)

Spray paint, silver

Bulky yarn (5) or super bulky yarn (6), yellow, 40 feet (12.2 m)

S hook

What You Do:

1. Begin by preparing the plastic container. Decide how tall you would like your planter to be, then use the permanent marker to make a straight line around the container at that height. Then draw a second line around the container 1 inch (2.5 cm) above that line (**A**).

   Tip: Wrap a rubber band around the plastic container at the height you would like your planter to be and use the rubber band as a straight-edge for drawing a line with the permanent marker.

2. Between the two lines, draw two triangles roughly 1 inch (2.5 cm) apart, using the photo as a guide (**B**).

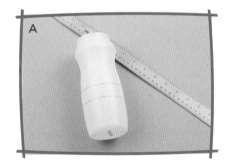

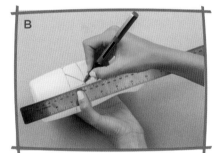

3. Using your shears, cut the plastic container along the lower line and along the edges of the triangles to form ears (**C**). Recycle the upper portion of the container.

4. Spray paint the outside of the container (**D**) and allow plenty of time to dry.

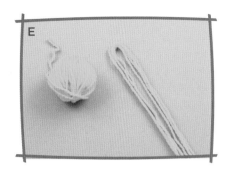

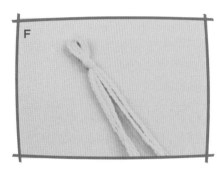

5. To make the macramé holder, cut four strands of yarn measuring 10 feet (3 m) each.

6. Line up the ends of all the strands, then fold in half (E).

7. Tie a knot at the folded end approximately 1½ inches (4 cm) from the fold (F).

8. You now have eight strands. Separate them into four pairs of two.

9. Take a moment to consider how low you would like the top of your planter to sit. Tie a knot in one of the pairs at this height.

10. Tie a knot at the same place in the remaining three pairs (G).

11. Now divide the pairs into new pairs. Moving clockwise, take a strand on the right side and pair with the strand to its right, tying them in a knot 2½ inches (6 cm) below the previous knot. Continue until all strands have been knotted. The final pair to be knotted will be the strand on the far left with the strand on the far right (H).

12. Tie a knot using all 8 strands 2 inches (5 cm) below those knots (I).

13. Fill the planter with soil and the plant of your choice. Nestle the planter into the bottom of the macramé hanger with the large knot beneath (J). Hang your new macramé planter from an S hook.

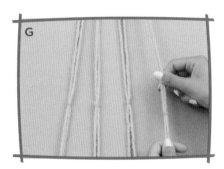

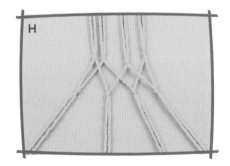

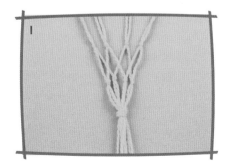

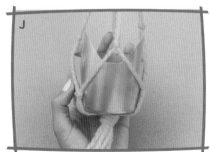

Purr-ty Painted Rocks

If you're not ready for the responsibility of a real pet cat, these cheerful
pet rocks are the just the companions you've been looking for!

What You Need:

Assorted rocks of various
shapes and sizes

Soap and water

Acrylic paint in a variety
of colors

Paint brushes

Pencil

Templates (page 103)

Permanent marker

Decoupage medium

*Note: This is a fun and easy creative project! As you're designing,
keep in mind that a lot of inspiration can come from the rocks
themselves—a skinny cat on a narrow rock or a fluffy cat
on a more rounded one. There is no wrong way to do this! The
more variety there is from stone to stone, the better the group will
look. If you need a little help getting started, use any or
all of the three included templates.*

What You Do:

1. Wash the rocks with soap and water and allow them to dry.

2. Paint the rock in a background color, if desired. Let dry.
   Use the pencil to draw a variety of cat imagery over each
   stone, or transfer the templates to the rocks if desired **(A)**.
   For a reminder on working with templates and transferring
   designs, see page x.

3. Paint on the images with your acrylic paints **(B)**. (Be sure to
   rinse your brush whenever you switch colors.)

4. If you'd like to define the images a little more or just add
   some additional details, you can trace around the shapes
   you've painted with a permanent marker.

5. Finish by covering in the decoupage medium to protect the
   design **(C)**. Let dry fully.

Embroidery Hoop Wall Hangings

Embroidery hoops and fabric are a great interior decorating project made all the better with a pop of color and some catty charm.

What You Need:

Pencil

Template (page 103)

Cardstock, 8½ x 11 inches (21.5 x 28 cm)

Scissors

Masking tape

3 embroidery hoops, in various sizes

Spray paint, in color of your choice

Fabric, enough to fill each of your embroidery hoops

Glue gun

What You Do:

1. Use the template to draw a pair of ears onto the cardstock. You will need one pair per embroidery hoop **(A)**. (Reduce or enlarge the template depending on the size of your embroidery hoop.) For a reminder on working with templates and transferring designs, see page x.

2. Cut out the ears **(B)**.

3. Wrap a small piece of masking tape around the hardware at the top of the hoop to protect it from the paint **(C)**.

4. Spray-paint the ears and the outer ring of the embroidery hoops **(D)**. Allow to dry completely. Remove the masking tape.

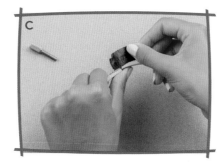
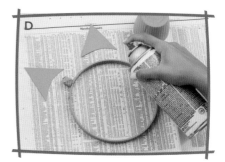

5. For each embroidery hoop, cut a piece of fabric that is 1 inch (2.5 cm) wider in diameter than the outer hoop **(E)**.

6. Place the fabric into the embroidery hoops and tighten the hardware. If needed, trim the fabric so there is only ½ inch (12 mm) of excess.

7. Fold the excess fabric to the wrong side and glue to the interior of the hoop **(F)**.

8. On the backside of the hoop, glue an ear to each side of the hoop's metal hardware **(G)**. Arrange on the wall as desired.

"You've Cat to be Kitten Me" Lampshade

Add a lot of personality to your home décor with this cute cat lampshade.
It will literally light up the room!

What You Need:

Round lampshade

Newspaper

Pencil

Scissors

Fabric, enough to go all the way around your lampshade

Template (page 106)

Pen

Fabric paint, in white, black, and pink

Paint brush

Spray mount

Glue

What You Do:

1. Place the lampshade on its side near the left edge of the newspaper (A).

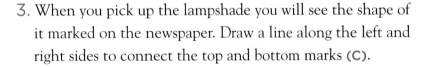

2. Start at the lampshade's seam and roll it to the right, across the newspaper, while simultaneously marking the top edge of the shade with a pen until you have arrived back at the seam. Now roll back in the opposite direction, to mark the bottom edge of the shade (B).

3. When you pick up the lampshade you will see the shape of it marked on the newspaper. Draw a line along the left and right sides to connect the top and bottom marks (C).

4. Measure ½ inch (12 mm) above the top line and ½ inch (12 mm) below the bottom line, and draw a new line around the initial shape, as shown. This will be your seam allowance (D). (This excess fabric will wrap around the shade's edges.)

5. Cut out the newspaper along the outer lines and trace this shape onto the wrong side of your fabric (E).

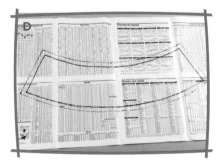

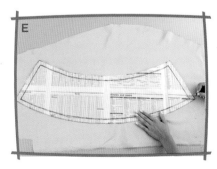

6. Cut the fabric out along the lines (F).

7. Place the template on top of the right side of your fabric, positioning it just above the middle. Trace the outline onto the fabric. For a reminder on working with templates and transferring designs, see page x.

8. Paint on the details (pupils, nose, and whiskers) as shown (G). Allow plenty of time to dry.

9. Spray the lampshade well with spray mount (H).

10. Place the lampshade on the backside of the fabric. Line up the lampshade seam with the mark on the left side (I) and roll to the right until you reach the mark on that side (J).

   Note: If you notice any wrinkles or bubbles forming, gently lift the fabric back up and smooth before continue to roll around the lampshade.

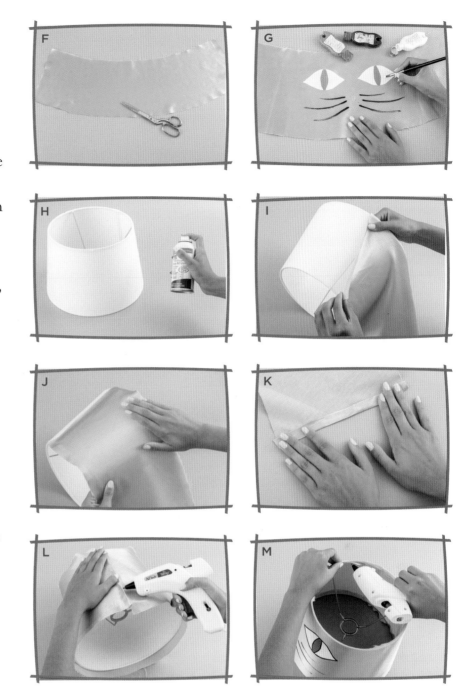

11. Fold the excess fabric at the seam under ½ inch (12 mm) toward the wrong side (K); glue onto the lampshade (L).

12. Fold the excess fabric at the top to the inside of the lampshade and glue in place (M).

13. Repeat step 11 with the excess fabric on the bottom of the lampshade.

Jewelry Tray

This sweet little tray is a great way to keep track of your rings and earrings and other small pieces of jewelry.

What You Need:

Rolling pin (or glass jar)

Air-dry clay, 3 ounces (85 g)

Template (page 106)

Knife

Dull pencil

Acrylic paint, in dark blue and white or colors of your choice

Paint brushes

Decoupage medium

Note: Be aware that drying times on air-dry clay can vary immensely, so this project will likely be done in two phases.

What You Do:

1. Using a rolling pin, flatten your clay so that is a little more than ⅛ inch (3 mm) thick and wider than the template (A).

2. Place the template over the clay. Use the knife to cut away all excess clay from the edges of the template (B).

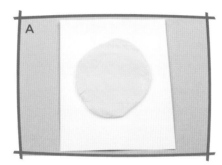
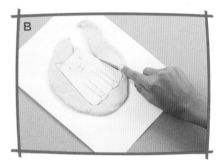

3. Use the pencil to trace over each of the template's details. A dull pencil will leave an impression in the clay without piercing the template (C).

4. Remove the template from the clay, then, using your thumb and index finger, pinch and raise the edge all around the perimeter of the clay until the piece looks like a dish (D).

Note: If some of the details are rubbed away while you are raising the edge, just go back over them with the pencil.

5. Follow the clay manufacturer's instructions for air-drying. This is likely to take at least a day if not more.

6. Once it's completely dry, use the acrylic paint to decorate the tray **(E)**. I used dark blue to paint the bottom and edges of the tray and white to paint the nose, paws, and small lines for fur. I outlined the legs, ears, eyes, whiskers, nose, and mouth with dark blue. Allow the paint to dry completely.

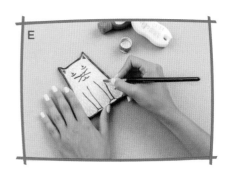

7. Finish by applying a layer of decoupage medium to the entire project to seal **(F)**. Allow time to dry before using.

Entertaining

The happy, colorful, festive projects in this section are just the thing for setting the mood at your next gathering. Whether you want to go for a full cat-themed soirée or are just looking to add a few cheerful feline touches, you'll find what you're looking for here.

Purr-fect Place Card

Make as many of these cute place cards as you need; you can keep and reuse them at future gatherings, or gift them as a happy addition to the guests' take-home party favors.

What You Need:

Pencil

Ruler

Scissors

Decorative paper, 5 x 10 inches (12.5 x 25.5 cm)

Googly eyes, ¼ inch (6 mm) in diameter

White paper

Glue

Pen

Double-sided tape (optional)

What You Do:

1. Cut the papers into the following pieces (A):

   - Decorative paper: 1 rectangle 3 x 7 inches (7.5 x 17.5 cm) and 2 strips ½ x 1½ inches (12 mm x 4 cm) each
   - White paper: 1 rectangle 1 x 3 inches (2.5 x 7.5 cm) and 2 strips ⅛ x 2 inches (3 mm x 5 cm) each

2. Set aside all of the pieces except for the large rectangle on decorative paper. Glue the two short sides of the large rectangle together with a ½ inch (12 mm) overlap (B) and allow to dry.

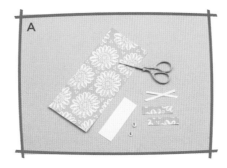

3. Push down on the edges of the tube as shown (C). Place a small drop of glue just below this spot to adhere the two sides.

4. Glue the googly eyes onto the side without the seam. Crisscross the two skinny white strips and glue them below the eyes to create whiskers (D).

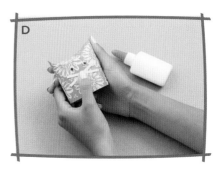

5. Cut a rounded edge into one of the short sides of both of the two remaining decorative paper strips (**E**).

6. Glue the two decorative paper strips to the short sides of the white rectangle so that ½ inch (12 mm) of the decorative paper strip overlaps on each side. Fold back the excess and glue it to the back (**F**).

7. Write the name of one of your guests, then glue to the front of the cat (**G**).

   Note: If you're planning to keep and reuse, swap double-sided tape for the glue in step 7 so that the names can be changed in the future as needed.

Party Plates

These cheerful plates set the stage for celebrating, and they could not be quicker
or easier to create! Try mixing and matching with the same decorative papers used for
the place cards (page 81) to give your table settings an extra pop of color.

What You Need:

Decorative papers, 4 x 4 inches
(10 x 10 cm)

Pencil

Scissors

Templates (page 106)

Nontoxic craft glue

Paper plates

What You Do:

1. On the backside of your decorative papers, trace the
template twice and cleanly cut out each piece **(A, B)**. For
a reminder on working with templates and transferring
designs, see page x.

2. Using the craft glue, affix the two triangles to the top of the
plates as pictured, approximately 3 inches (7.5 cm) apart **(C)**.

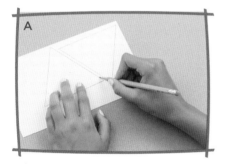

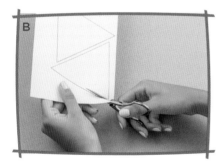

Cozy Kitten Drink Koozie

Cool cats for your cold drinks. Try changing the cat's eye color
on each koozie you make as a colorful and creative way for friends
to distinguish which drink belongs to whom.

What You Need:

Templates (page 107)

Pen

Craft foam, 3 x 5 inches
(7.5 x 12.5 cm), in black,
white, blue, and yellow

Scissors

Permanent marker

Drink koozie

Glue

What You Do:

1. Use the templates to cut
all of the shapes from
craft foam. For a reminder
on working with templates
and transferring designs,
see page x.

2. Snip the middle of the gray rectangle, leaving ¼ inch (6 mm)
at one end uncut. Trim the uncut side into a point (A).

3. Use a permanent marker to draw an elongated black pupil in
the middle of the colored foam circles (B).

4. Glue the circles in the center of the white eye shapes to
make eyes.

5. Glue all of the foam pieces onto the koozie so that it looks
like a cat, as shown (C).

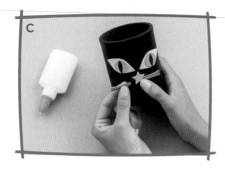

Paw-sitively Pretty Bunting

What do you get when you mix metallic-gold paper with hearts, diamonds, rhinestones, and hot-pink fringe trim? Over-the-top decorating in the best way possible. If this doesn't put your guests in a celebratory mood, nothing will!

What You Need:

Templates (page 107)

Pencil

Scissors

2 sheets metallic-gold paper, 12 x 12 inches (30 x 30 cm)

2 sheets pink paper, 12 x 12 inches (30 x 30 cm)

Glue

Hole punch

Paper brads (3 per pair of cats)

8 small rhinestones, ⅛ inch (3 mm) wide

Decorative fringe, 5 feet (1.5 m)

Note: This amount of paper makes up to 10 cats. If you'd like your bunting to be even longer, use more sheets of metallic-gold and pink paper.

What You Do:

1. The cats are created in pairs. Use the templates to trace and cut out the following pieces **(A)**.

   - Metallic paper: 2 cat bodies, 2 cat heads for each pair
   - Pink paper: 1 heart, 2 diamonds (fold the diamonds where indicated) for each pair

2. Use the hole punch to make holes where shown on the template: the top-front paw of each cat, the back-bottom paws, the center-top portion of the heart, and the two indicated points on each diamond.

3. Glue the cats' heads to the bodies as shown **(B)**.

4. Decorate all of the cats' faces by gluing on the rhinestone eyes and crisscrossed whiskers made from thin strips of the pink paper **(C)**.

5. Insert one of the brads through the heart, then through each of the front paw holes, and open the brad's prongs in the back to secure **(D)**.

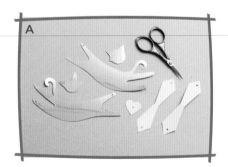

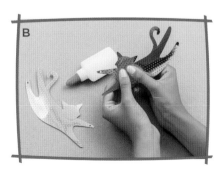

6. The two cats are now attached, facing each other (E).

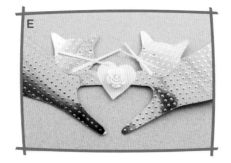

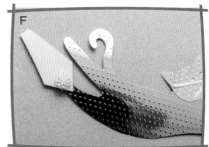

7. At the left edge of the bunting, insert a brad through one of the diamond holes and the back paw on the leftmost cat, then fold the diamond to insert the brad through the back. Open the prongs to secure (F).

8. To add more pairs of cats, insert a brad through a diamond, the back paw on the rightmost cat, the back paw of a new cat facing to the right, and through the other half of the folded diamond. Open the prongs to secure (G).

9. Continue adding pairs of cats until the bunting has reached your desired length.

10. To finish, repeat step 7 but this time on the far-right side.

11. Insert the fringe trim through the fold in all of the diamond shapes, leaving plenty of excess on the right and left sides (H).

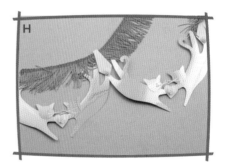

Festive Feline Fans

Hanging paper fans are another festive decoration to set the mood for a party.
This super-fast project employs just a few steps to transform standard
paper fans into fantastic felines.

What You Need:

Hanging paper fans, at least 2

Scissors

Glue

Sheet of white paper,
   8½ x 11 inches (21.5 x 28 cm)

Rhinestone, ⅜ inch (1 cm) wide

What You Do:

1. From one of the paper fans, cut away a segment of approximately 5 to 6 pleats **(A)**.

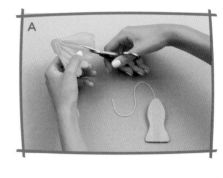

2. Cut this piece in half **(B)**.

3. Open the segments and glue on the backside of the fan at the top-right and left sides **(C)**. These are the ears.

4. Add whiskers by cutting three long, thin strips of the white paper **(D)**.

5. Form an "X" with the three strips and glue them together at the intersection.

6. Glue the whiskers to the intersection directly atop the fan's midpoint.

7. Finish by gluing a rhinestone "nose" over the top-center of the whiskers **(E)**.

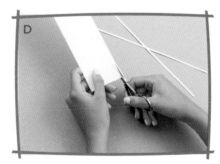

Templates

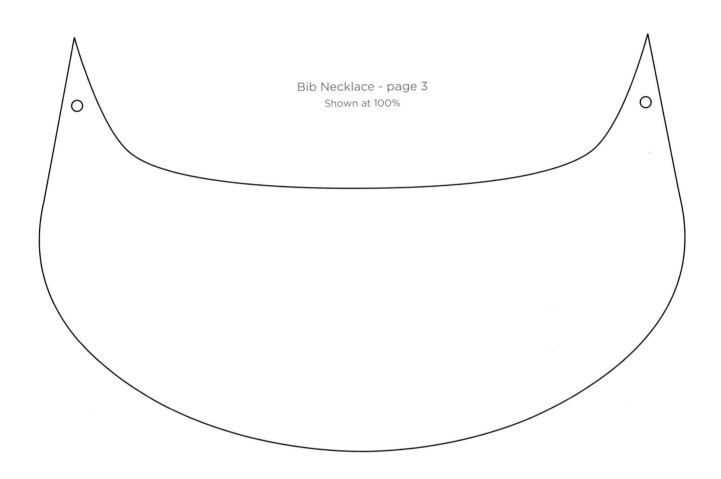

Bib Necklace - page 3
Shown at 100%

Cat Ring - page 4
Shown at 100%

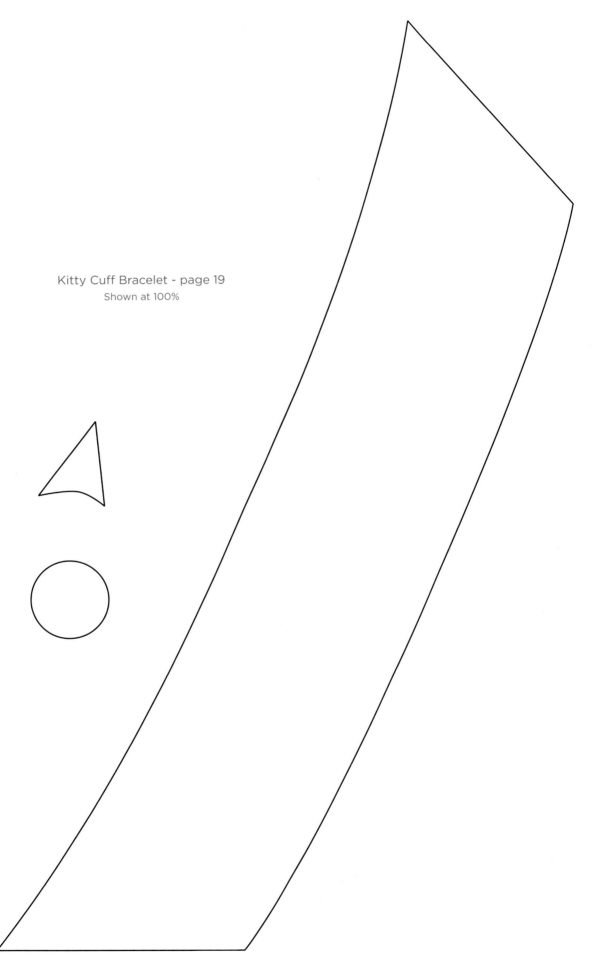

Kitty Cuff Bracelet - page 19
Shown at 100%

Cat Wallet, Template A - page 17
Shown at 100%

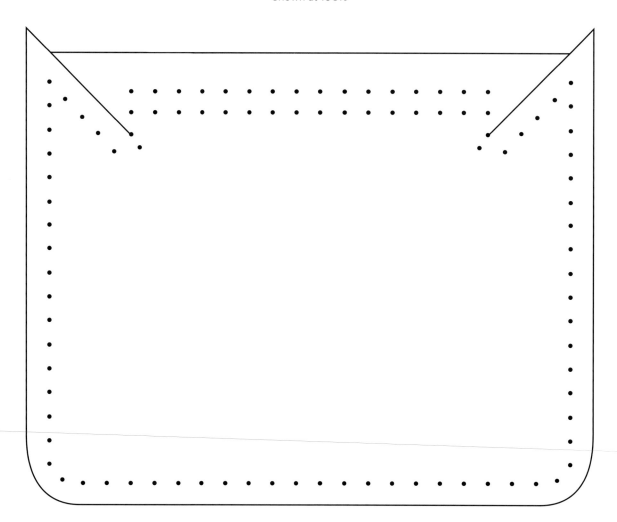

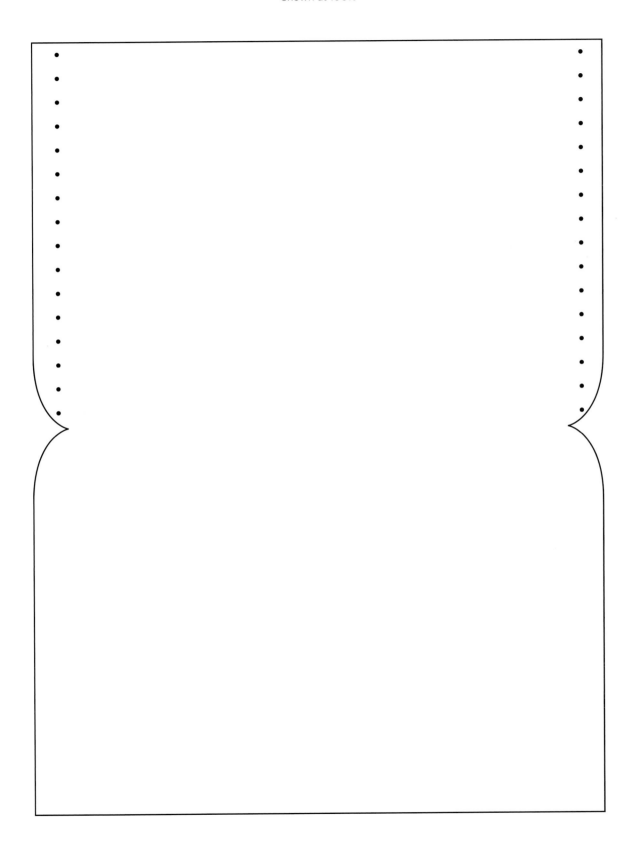

Paw Print Sneakers - page 23
Shown at 100%

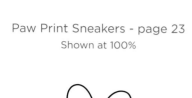

Elbow Patches - page 31
Shown at 100%

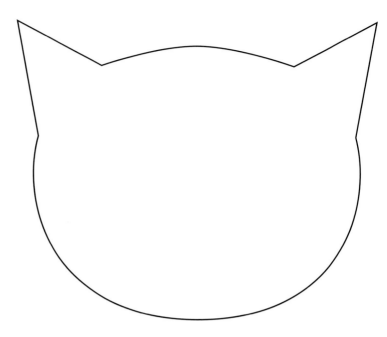

Thigh-High Socks - page 29
Shown at 100%

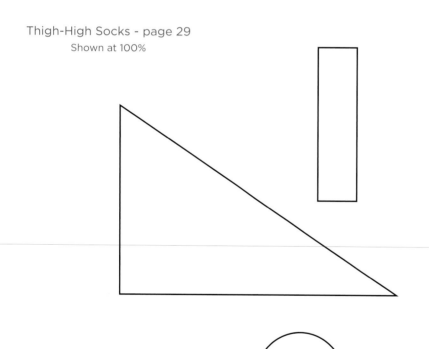

"Look at Me Meow"
Bejeweled Collar - page 32
Shown at 100%

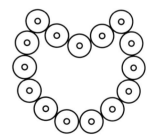

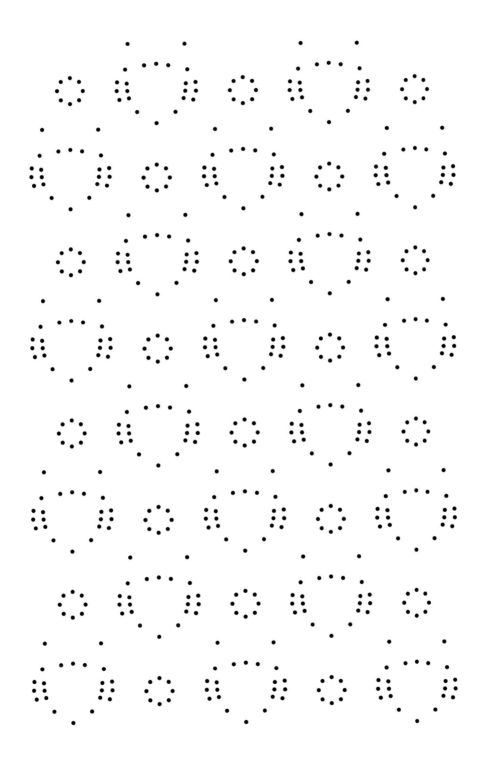

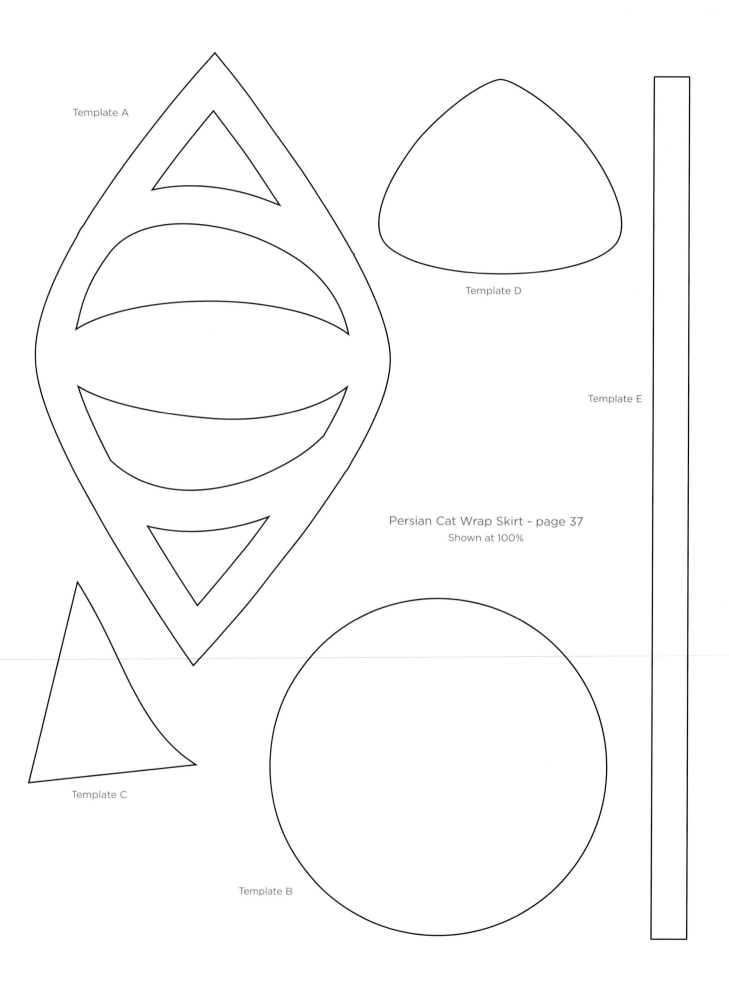

Template A

Template D

Template E

Persian Cat Wrap Skirt - page 37
Shown at 100%

Template C

Template B

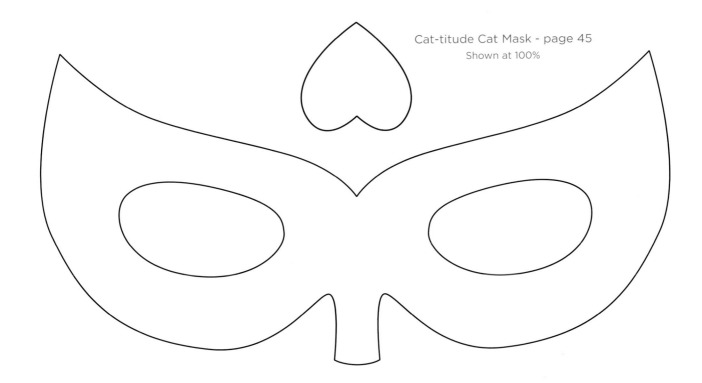

Cat-titude Cat Mask - page 45
Shown at 100%

Su-purr-ior Stationery - page 52
Shown at 100%

Su-purr-ior Stationery - page 52
Shown at 100%

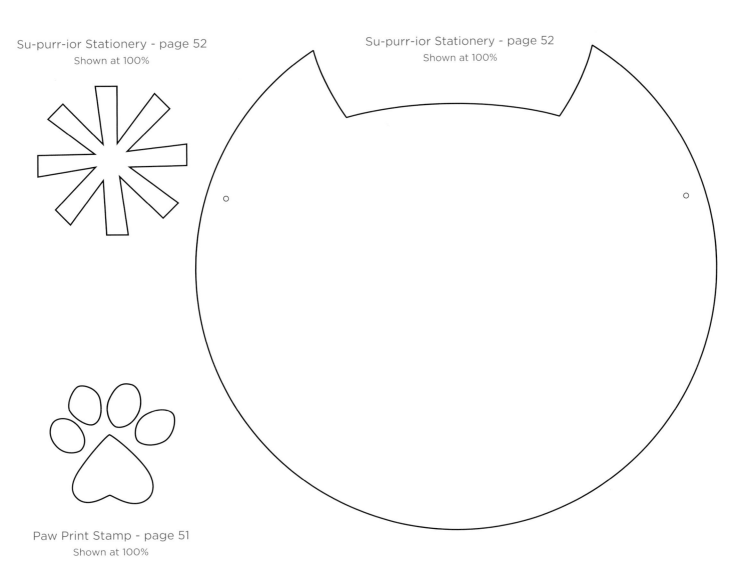

Paw Print Stamp - page 51
Shown at 100%

Feline Felt Storage Bin - page 55
Enlarge by 200% (small box)

Feline Felt Storage Bin - page 55
Shown at 100% (small box)

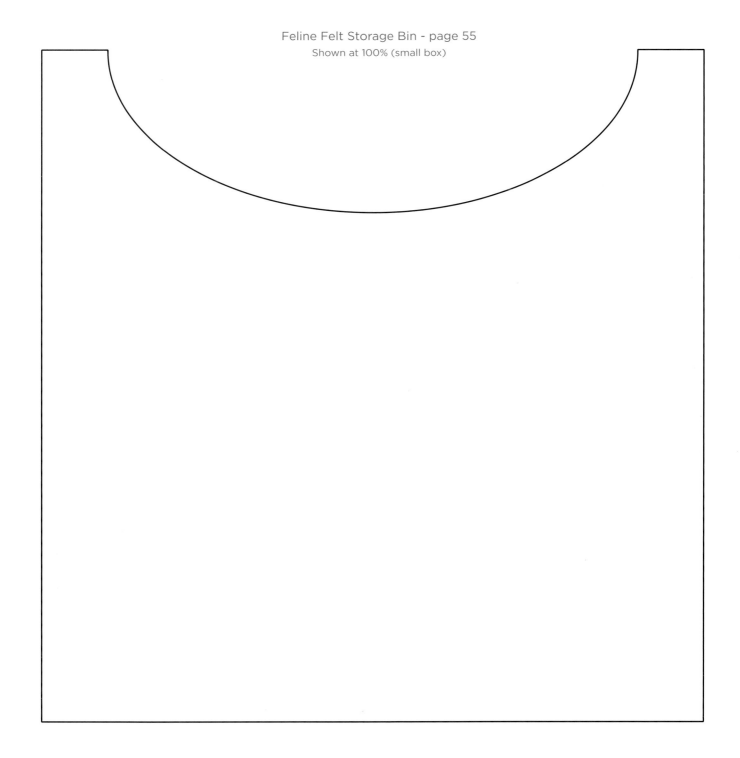

Purr-ty Painted Rocks - page 69
Shown at 100%

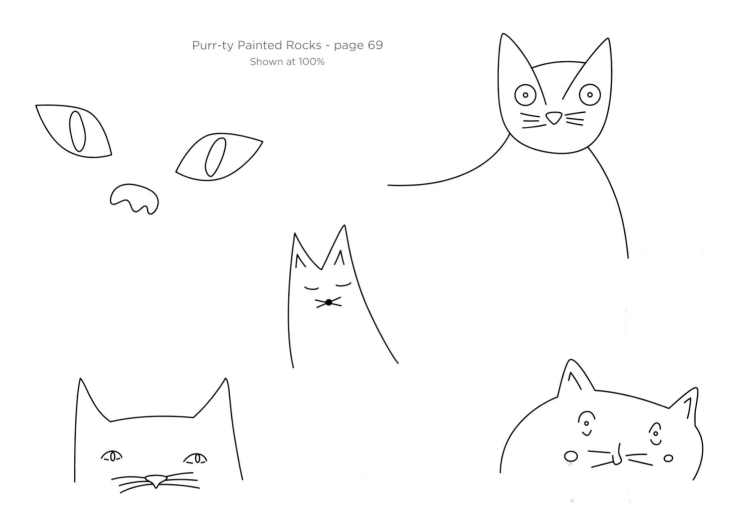

Embroidery Hoop Wall Hangings - page 70
Shown at 100%

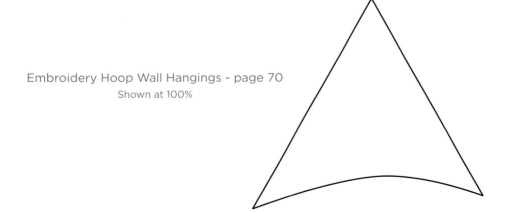

Cat Nap Throw Pillow - page 63
Enlarge by 125%

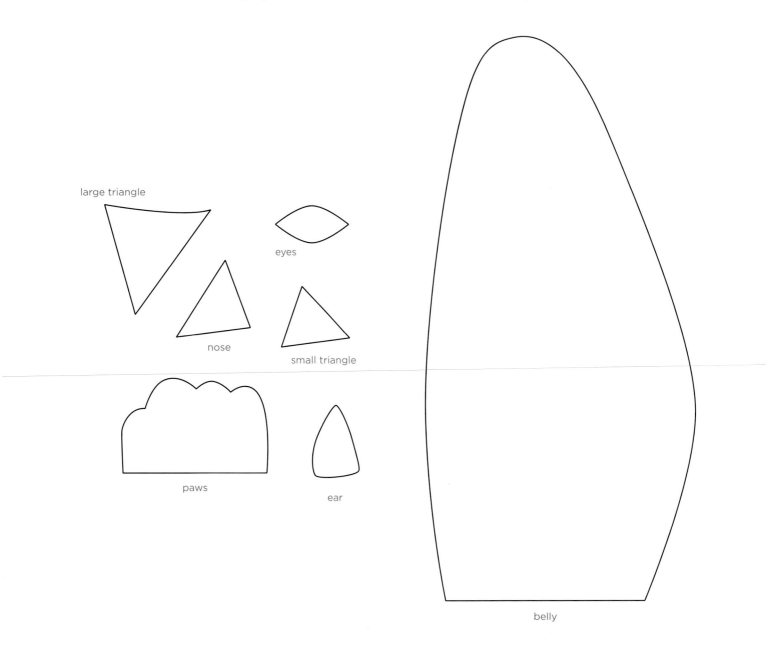

large triangle

eyes

nose

small triangle

paws

ear

belly

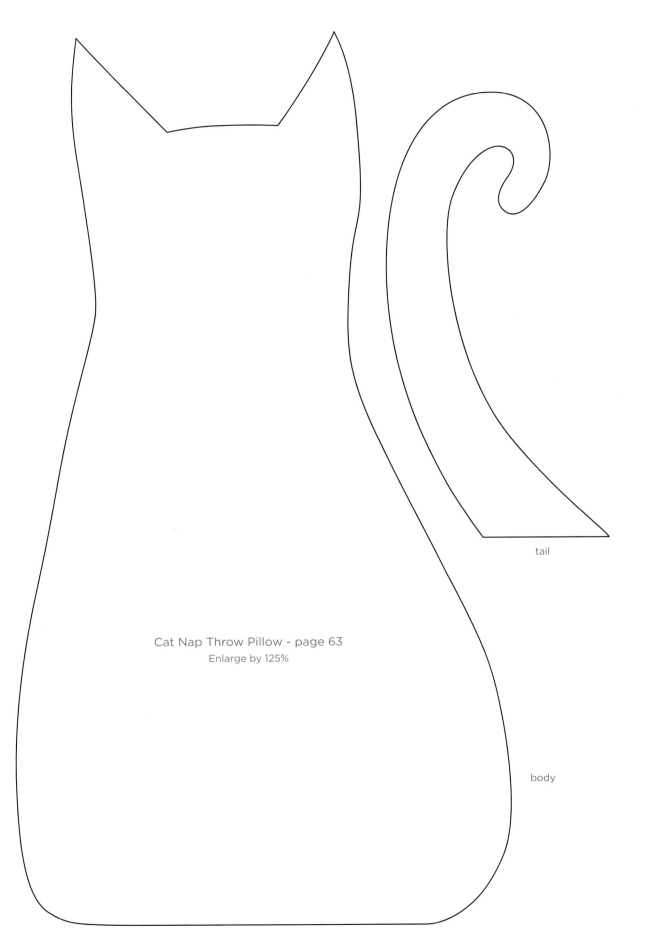

Cat Nap Throw Pillow - page 63
Enlarge by 125%

tail

body

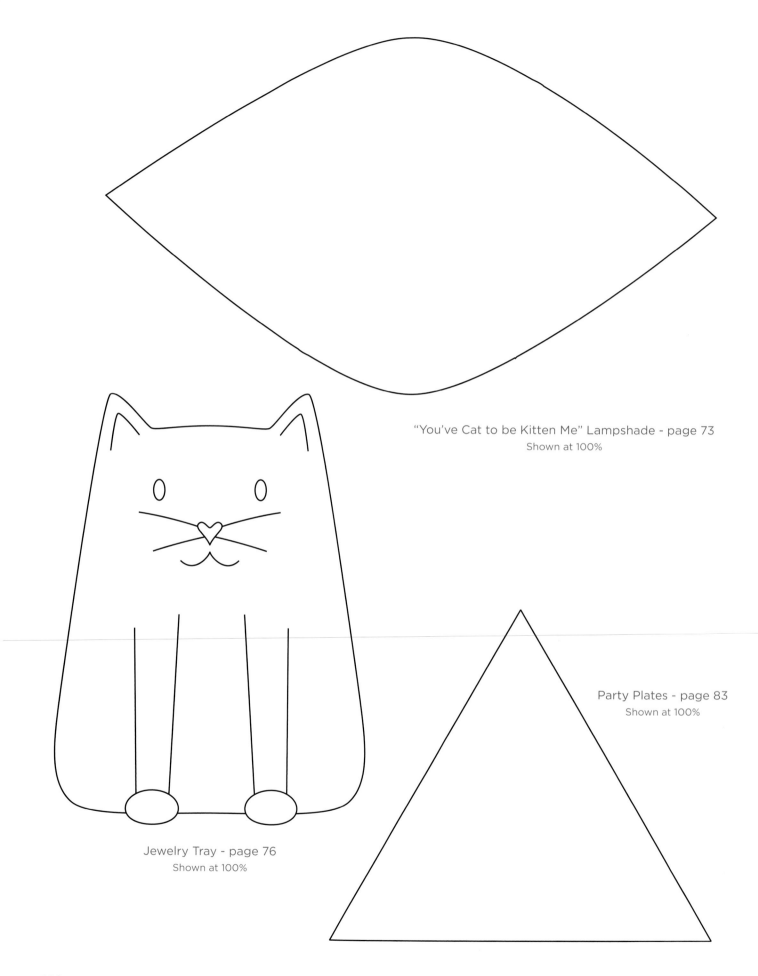

"You've Cat to be Kitten Me" Lampshade - page 73
Shown at 100%

Party Plates - page 83
Shown at 100%

Jewelry Tray - page 76
Shown at 100%

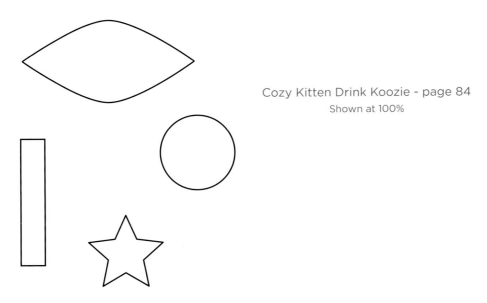

Cozy Kitten Drink Koozie - page 84
Shown at 100%

Paw-sitively Pretty Bunting - page 86
Shown at 100%

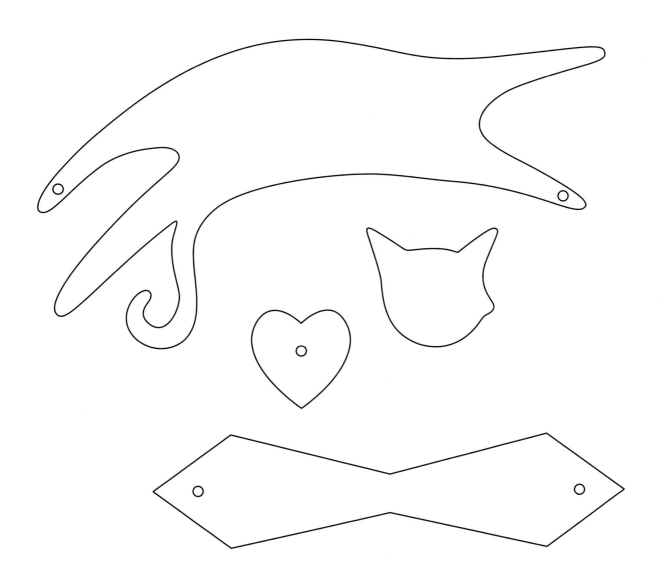

About the Author

Kat Roberts is the co-author of *Loom Band It: 60 Rubberband Projects for the Budding Loomineer*, *Make It by the Book*, and *Friendship Bracelets*. She maintains a blog called *We Can Re-Do It* (wecanredoit.blogspot.com) that offers a wide variety of original craft projects with step-by-step instructions. She lives in Brooklyn, New York.

About the Cats

No cats were harmed in the making of this book!

Misty Stack is a sweet and friendly two-year-old tuxedo cat from New Jersey. She was adopted after determinedly stalking her family for days, eventually climbing up a kitchen-window screen and dangling there, meowing maniacally, while the family ate dinner. Misty happily introduces herself to every visitor with the hope of receiving a scratch under her chin. She loves bird-watching, felted-wool cat toys, and sharpening her claws on the living-room couch. Her loud meows match the volume of her boisterous adopted family.

General Jeb Stuart, a.k.a. Jeb is a 3½-year-old Russian Blue mix from Dumont, NJ. Unlike his aggressive namesake, Jeb is a sweet and gentle love bug who demands that his daddy brush him and mommy give him belly rubs and kisses each morning before work. Jeb's favorite toy is a stemmed, golden sunflower that he stole from mommy's wreath. He is a cancer survivor.

Milo J. Brown is a fifteen-year-old longtime resident of Baldwinsville, NY. He is a Virgo who loves sliced turkey and sitting on laps. His favorite toy was a stuffed sock monkey (now deceased), and his favorite pastime is tied between drinking water from the faucet and dunking his head under a running showerhead. He always makes sure to locate the nearest carpet right before getting sick and, although far from "basic," loves anything pumpkin flavored. Named for the cat counterpart in *The Adventures of Milo and Otis*, Milo has long upheld his position in the local neighborhood watch by hissing and chasing all suspicious birds, squirrels, and boyfriends. While he loves his whole family (Janice, Scott, and Ashley), his special person—Lindsey—is the only one who gets to kiss him right on the nose.

Acknowledgments

I have so many people who had a role in bringing this book to life to thank!

First and foremost, I'd like to thank the wonderful duo of Kate McKean and Connie Santisteban, whose enthusiasm and belief in this project right from the start took it from just a funny idea to an actual book. I can't overstate how integral these two women were to every step of this process. I'm so grateful to have them in my corner.

My most sincere gratitude to the entire team at Lark Crafts, who made this experience every bit as fun as I hoped it would be. Wendy, Jo, Lorie, Shannon, and Chris—each of them is so terrific at what they do that I feel beyond lucky for the opportunity to work with them. And thank you to the models: Jill, Kelsey, and Julia, you made everything look so good!

Huge thanks to my supportive and patient family. My daughter, Ophelia, a badass crafter herself and constant source of inspiration. My partner in life and love, Fiffe—thank you for remaining calm and kind even when every square inch of our apartment was covered with some sort of cat-related crafting material. And, of course, my mom, for her constant enthusiasm and being the best materials sourcer I've ever met.

And last, though certainly not least, to my sweet dog, Sharker, for being remarkably understanding throughout this entire process. She's the baddest.

Every single one of you are the cat's pajamas. Thank you so, so much!

Index

Note: Page numbers in *italics* indicate projects and (templates).

6-17
d